Instructional Design Competencies: The Standards

•

Third Edition

Rita C. Richey
Wayne State University

Dennis C. Fields
St. Cloud State University

Marguerite Foxon
Motorola, Inc.

With

Robert C. Roberts, Timothy Spannaus, and J. Michael Spector

ERIC ® Clearinghouse on Information & Technology
Syracuse University – Syracuse, New York
IR-111
March, 2001

Instructional Design Competencies: The Standards

Third edition

Rita C. Richey, Ed.
Wayne State University
Dennis C. Fields
St. Cloud State University
Marguerite Foxon
Motorola, Inc.

with
Robert C. Roberts, Timothy Spannaus, and J. Michael Spector

This edition is published by the ERIC Clearinghouse on Information & Technology in cooperation with the International Board of Standards for Training, Performance and Instruction (IBSTPI).

ISBN: 0-937597-52-X

ERIC Clearinghouse on Information & Technology
Syracuse University
621 Skytop Road, Suite 160
Syracuse, NY 13244-5290
1-800-464-9107
www.ericit.org
IR-111

U. S. Department of Education
Office of Educational Research and Improvement
National Library of Education

This product was funded in part with Federal funds from the U.S. Department of Education under contract no. ED-99-CO-0005. The content of this publication does not necessarily reflect the views or policies of the U.S. Department of Education nor does mention of trade names, commercial products, or organizations imply endorsement by the U.S. government. The U.S. Department of Educationís web address is: http://www.ed.gov.

R. D. Lankes, Director, ERIC Clearinghouse on Information & Technology
Eric Plotnick, Associate Director, ERIC Clearinghouse on Information & Technology
Susann L. Wurster, Publications Coordinator
Tammy L. DiDomenico, Copy Editor
Lloyd J. Lathrop, Jr., Designer

Printed in Syracuse, New York, U.S.A.   March 2001.

This book is dedicated to Barry Bratton

1944 – 1997

Associate Professor of Instructional Technology,
The University of Iowa
Chair, Task Force for ID Certification
1978-1983
First President, International Board of Standards for
Training, Performance and Instruction

Barry, we think of you often and your work goes on.

We would like to acknowledge the contributions of the many persons who have participated in the development and validation of these newly revised instructional design competencies. Each member of the IBSTPI Board has participated in the process. In addition three former Board members were involved in the process – Peter Dean, George Pollard, and Dennis Sheriff, the past president of the International Board of Standards for Training, Performance and Instruction.

These competencies have also been influenced by the many persons who provided input and reactions – both formally and informally – throughout the long development process. We thank you all.

Table of Contents

Part II - The IBSTPI ID Competencies: Validation

List of Tables

List of Figures

Foreword

The International Board of Standards for Training, Performance and Instruction (IBSTPI) is a professional service organization to the instructional design, training and performance improvement communities. The Board serves these communities through research, publications and conferences.

The Board consists of 15 professionals, selected to be broadly representative of the communities we serve. Members are from universities, government, large businesses and consulting firms. In recent years, the Board has begun to live up to its name as an international board, with directors from Australia, Canada, England, Norway, The Netherlands, in addition to members from the United States.

Each board member serves as an exemplar of professional practice and the ethics of the profession. They serve as public advocates of the profession in speaking engagements, seminars, workshops and other public discussions. The Board seeks to portray professional practice as a set of agreed upon competencies for the various functions of the profession. The Board publishes ideal standard competencies for trainers, designers and managers who work in the profession of performance improvement. One intent of the Board is to have these standards adopted and used by a wider array of public and private organizations. The Board also arranges to update and revise standards of practices so they are more applicable across time and place.

History

The Board grew from the work of the Joint Certification Task Force, which was composed of the Association for Educational Communications and Technology (AECT) and the National Society for Performance and Instruction (NSPI, now the International Society for Performance Improvement, ISPI). Created in 1977, the Joint Task Force included over 30 professional practitioners and academics with expertise in various facets of training, performance and instruction. The Task Force developed the initial set of competencies for the instructional design professional, published an index linking current publications to competencies and created a prototype assessment procedure. Also, during this period, members of the Task Force spoke at professional meetings and published articles on professional competence and certification.

The Task Force reorganized itself in 1983 to avoid conflicts of interest with its parent organizations. This action was taken with the approval and encouragement of the Boards of Directors of NSPI, AECT, and the Division of Instructional Development within AECT.

Research and Development Activities

The Board places priority on research leading to publication of sets of competencies and associated performance statements, pertaining to knowledge, skills and attitudes associated with instructors, technical trainers, instructional designers, training managers and related professionals. The Board has also developed a Code of Ethical Standards for the profession and it is included in this volume. *Instructor Competencies : The Standards* (1993) is the basis for many instructor training programs and the Certified Technical Trainer and Certified Professional Development Trainer programs of The Chauncey Group International.

Conferences sponsored by the Board typically gather researchers, invited speakers and participants around a potential or existing set of competencies. The Board convened a conference at the University of Bergen (Norway) to look at the intersection of instructional design and performance improvement. A conference at Estes Park, Colorado (USA) considered revisions to the Training Manager Competencies. The Board is currently revising those competencies for publication in 2001. An upcoming IBSTPI conference, co-sponsored by Lancaster University (England), will focus on on-line teaching.

Further information about IBSTPI and its activities can be found at www.IBSTPI.org.

Timothy Spannaus, President
March, 2000

2000 IBSTPI Board Members

Ileana de le Teja,
    Associate Researcher.
    L'Informatique Cognitive et
    Environonnements de Formation
    Research Center, Télé-université,
    Quebec (Canada)
Patricia J. Douglas,
    Principal, IBM Global Services,
    International Business Machines
    (USA)
Dennis C. Fields,
    Professor, Information Media, St
    Cloud State University (USA)
Kristian Folkman,
    Senior Adviser,
    Telenor Corporate University
    (Norway)
Marguerite Foxon,
    Principal Performance
    Technologist, Motorola, Inc.
    (USA)
Peter Goodyear,
    Professor of Educational Research,
    Lancaster University (UK)
Sandra Quesada,
    Director, Global Training and
    Development, Eli Lilly and
    Company (USA)
Rita C. Richey,
    Professor and Program
    Coordinator, Instructional
    Technology, Wayne State
    University (USA)

Robert C. Roberts,
    Principal Consultant, Bob Roberts
    and Associates (USA)
Rod Sims,
    Associate Professor, School of
    Multimedia & Information
    Technology, Southern Cross
    University (Australia)
Timothy W. Spannaus,
    CEO and Chairman, The
    Emdicium Group, Inc. (USA)
J. Michael Spector, Professor and
    Chair, Instructional Design,
    Development & Evaluation,
    Syracuse University (USA) and
    Director, Educational Information
    Science & Technology, University
    of Bergen (Norway)
Mark S. Teachout,
    Executive Director, Learning &
    Performance Technology, USAA
    (USA)
Jelke van der Pal,
    Instructional Psychologist,
    Department of Man-Machine
    Integration, National Aerospace
    Laboratory (Netherlands)
Diane Wagner,
    Principal Consultant, DW
    Consulting (USA)

Preface

The Beginnings

In the late 1970's and early 1980's, Instructional Design (ID) as a field of practice was beginning to assert itself in the worlds of education and training. Corporations and the military had published landmark training development methodologies based on ID. Demand for qualified designers was substantial, and introductory textbooks were in wide use. While some professionals entered the field through graduate-level academic programs, the majority of ID practitioners received their training in work settings, from commercial seminars, internal training and mentoring. Theory for the new field emerged from a broad range of disciplines, and was only beginning to coalesce into a coherent body of knowledge. Every theoretician and practitioner, it seemed, had a different opinion about what ID was, a different Instructional Systems Design (ISD) model with different names for its activities, and thus, different opinions on what competence in ID really meant. At the same time, ID felt a need to differentiate – and even prove – itself in relation to the broad practice of education (especially curriculum development) and training (especially Human Resource Development).

In this environment, a group of academics and practitioners began meeting in 1977, under the auspices of the Association for Educational Communications and Technology (AECT) and the National Society for Performance and Instruction (now the International Society for Performance Improvement, ISPI). Under the leadership of Barry Bratton of the University of Iowa, the group began to grapple with many of the key questions essential to the identity and growth of the field:

- Is there such a thing as Instructional Design?
- Is ID a discipline, a field of practice, a profession, or a job task?
- Is there any core ID knowledge or competency other than one's favorite ISD model or technology of delivery?
- Given the broad range of terminology and conceptual structure in the field, *is* there a common core of knowledge and competency? If so, what literature defines it?
- If those core competencies exist, would someone possessing them behave in practice any different from someone trained in classroom teaching, training development, technical writing, HRD, or any given content area?
- If those core competencies exist, would two experts possessing them behave in practice in similar ways, or produce recognizably similar work products?
- If we can define core competencies for what ID *is*, will the same principles we use to include a core ID competency also allow us to define what a core competency for ID *is not?*
- *Should* we attempt to define a set of core competencies for ID?
- What will be the desirable (and undesirable) effects of doing so?
- What level of expertise should the competencies describe?
- What are the audiences for the competency definition? What needs of those audiences should the competencies try to meet?

In those still early years of the field, the answers to these questions were much less obvious than they are now. Work within the committee, and dialogues with the professional community surrounding the committee, made it clear that there was no consensus over whether a competency definition was feasible or desirable. A parallel debate on professional certification was even more controversial, and ultimately came to naught.

In light of the uncertainties and controversies surrounding the 1986 ID Competencies, it is interesting to see what their influence has been. I am aware of no formal data collection effort on use of the document, but as a co-author, inquiries and comments from a variety of sources have been addressed to me over the years. Based on these communications, it appears that many of the hopes of the original working group have been realized. The ID Competencies appear to have been used in these ways:

- As a basis for defining professional training programs, in academic programs and in some corporate settings;
- As a basis for job descriptions and role definitions in a variety of workplace settings;
- Through its bibliography, as a sourcebook for the core literature of the field;
- As an organizing structure for textbooks and knowledge bases; and
- As a means of explaining to consumers of ID services and development team members what "value added" an ID practitioner can bring to a project.

The reach of the ID Competencies has been world-wide, and it has found use by almost every sector of private enterprise, government, the military, and education. That IBSTPI continues its work after so many years is a testimony to the magnitude of the need for its work, including the ID competencies.

The Changes

It has been clear for some time that a revision of the original document was urgently needed. In nearly all of the underlying bodies of theory upon with ID draws, there have been major new developments in the past 15 years. At the same time, interest in, acceptance of, and expectations for the kinds of training and education developed by ID practitioners have all grown explosively. The conversion to a knowledge-based economy – still the prediction of futurists when the original document was published – is now a reality few would deny. Technology-based training and education now refers almost exclusively to computer and Internet-based technologies, and almost everyone is aware of their potential for transformative change.

In light of these dramatic changes, it is instructive to note both how the current working group has changed the ID Competencies, and how they have retained the intent of the original. The basic phases of the ISD process are still recognizable, though the substance of the competencies has changed somewhat. For example, while analysis of content structures is still important, writing objectives no longer stands as a separate core competency. Most remarkable is the differentiation of the competencies into Essential and Advanced. This represents an intent to broaden the usefulness of the competencies.

The 1986 Competencies were intended to describe a "journeyman" instructional designer: someone who may or may not have had formal academic training in the field, but probably did have considerable training and exposure to the literature of the field through whatever route. In addition, however, the level of proficiency described was taken to represent someone who would probably have at least three years of experience in the field, beyond entry-level training. The current revision takes this notion considerably further, in two ways. First, the revision discriminates between the essential and the advanced levels. Second, it discriminates between competencies which are universally recognized as required of all practitioners, and those which have broad, but not universal support. These designations will help extend the usefulness of the competencies to a broader range of application environments, and they will help make the competencies useful throughout one's professional career.

Almost equally remarkable is the addition of the section in the current edition called "Professional Foundations." This section explicitly recognizes the importance of a knowledge base for ID, and the professional responsibility practitioners have for career-long learning and update of that knowledge base. This recognition of knowledge as a foundation to practice was left implicit in the first version, due to its emphasis on exclusively performance-based definition of the competencies. The change signifies a maturing of scholarship in the field, as well as the influence of the transition from behavioral to cognitive learning theory underlying the field. The increased emphasis on ethics and diversity in the revision certainly are timely additions to a view of professional practice which is more rounded than in the original.

A topic of considerable debate in the original working group was the desirability of including competence in particular technologies, or families of technologies. Certainly, it was true then, and is perhaps even more true now, that ID practitioners work in technology-heavy environments and have technology expertise as part of their skill sets. Ultimately, however, the consensus of the original working group was that expertise in specific technologies, while common, was context-specific and thus not a core competency for the field. The current revision has found a way to recognize the importance of technological competence for the practitioner, while continuing to recognize both the volatility and the context-specificity of expertise with any particular technology. This is clearly an improvement.

The section now called Implementation and Management represents a considerable strengthening of the intent of the original. This represents both a better awareness of the role these competencies play in ID, and also the increasing importance of ID in the success of knowledge-based enterprises, especially in business environments.

In sum, the current revision positions the competencies well for continued growth of the field. It continues to recognize the diverse career paths which lead people into the field as well as the range of contexts in which ID is practiced. At the same time, it strongly recognizes the core knowledge and principles of the field, and provides for their growth. There is every reason to believe that the revision's influence on the field will be even more substantial than was true of the first version.

Wellesley R. ("Rob") Foshay,
Vice President, Instructional Design and Cognitive Learning
PLATO Learning, Inc.
Rfoshay@plato.com
Naperville, Illinois
March, 2000

PART I

The IBSTPI ID Competencies: Development, Interpretation and Application

Chapter 1

Instructional Design Competence

In 1986, the International Board of Standards for Training, Performance and Instruction published the first edition of *Instructional Design Competencies: The Standards*. This was the culmination of work that began in 1978. Drafts of the initial designer competency list evolved from 1979 through 1983 (Task Force on ID Certification, 1981). In retrospect, this work occurred in the infancy (or at least the toddler years) of the practice of instructional design (ID). In this volume IBSTPI is presenting its second view of the competencies of instructional designers. It is a greatly expanded view that reflects the complexities of current practice and technology, theoretical advancements, and the social tenor of the times. Nonetheless, it is a view that is still rooted in the traditional notion of design competence.

This chapter lays the foundation for the new IBSTPI ID competencies. It briefly summarizes the changes in design practice since 1978 and then examines the IBSTPI competency development model and the assumptions central to the new competencies. This model provides a structure for not only empirically based development, but also for competency definition at varying degrees of detail and specificity.

Instructional Design: Yesterday and Today

Instructional design has multiple origins. Theoretically, it is rooted in theories of general systems, learning, communications, and instruction (Richey, 1986), and its practice origins are in the military training demands of World War II (Dick, 1989; Seels, 1989). Gustafson and Branch (1997) credit the Barson model used at Michigan State University between 1961 and 1965 as being one of the first ID models. However, it was not until the 1970's that the term "instructional design" was even commonly used. Instead, most "designers" called themselves educational psychologists, or media specialists, or training specialists (Dick, 1989). Dick and Carey's now-classic book, *The Systematic Design of Instruction*, was not published until 1978 – only one year before the first draft of the original IBSTPI ID competencies.

For the most part, the early ID models had a product orientation. The model was directed toward the design and development of a product, but not the implementation and maintenance of that product in a given environment. With the exception of the work of Leonard Silvern, these design projects occurred either in a higher education setting or produced instruction for elementary or secondary schools.

Since the 1980's, the preponderance of instructional design (ID) practice has occurred within the private sector, primarily in business and industrial settings. This coincides with the steady growth of employee training as an integral part of most organizations. In the United States alone, the training industry was a $62.5 billion endeavor in 1999, up from the 1990 estimate of $45.5 billion and a 1985 estimate of $30 billion as reported by the American Society of Training and Development (Industry Report, 1999; Industry Report, 1990). Remarkably, these data are only partially descriptive, since they reflect only the direct cost of formal training in organizations with 100 or more employees. Informal, on-the-job training is not included. Training in smaller firms throughout the United States is not included. Moreover, such growth is not unique to the United States, but is duplicated to a great extent worldwide.

This growth reflects an emphasis not simply on producing a more knowledgeable workforce, but increasingly upon improving employee on-the-job performance and solving organizational problems. Correspondingly in today's market, instructional design to many is not merely an organized approach to product or course development, but is instead a generic process for analyzing human performance problems and determining appropriate solutions to such problems. In addition, designers and training managers must often predict future problems and likely organizational changes and project ways to prepare employees for these new situations (Pieters, 1997). It is this dominant orientation that serves as the foundation of these new IBSTPI design competencies.

Not only did the setting of this new design activity change from the early years, but there were also changes in the conditions under which designers worked. No longer did designers work primarily alone, but now design teams predominate, especially in large organizations. Often designers serve as external consultants or suppliers. The new technologies have drastically changed design tools and processes. The changes have been matched by increased pressures to reduce the time required for design and development, even as designers are now expected to prove their effectiveness by demonstrating they have a positive impact on the mission and profits of the organization.

This new work environment has stimulated changes in design tools and techniques, and correspondingly in the expansion of designer expertise. The basic 1970's skills have been supplemented by new technology skills, business acumen, and more sophisticated evaluation skills, for example. Designer career ladders are developing to match these new skills.

In today's design market, the field is no longer primarily an American endeavor. Instructional designers are working and being educated worldwide. As organizations expand beyond individual country boundaries, designers are addressing the issues of preparing and adapting instructional materials for different cultures. This is done both internationalizing the materials to make them "culture-free" and by localizing the products to make them "culturally dependent" (Richey and Morrison, 2000).

Instructional designers, like others employed in the 21st century, are faced with the prospect of continual re-tooling to meet their new job demands. Even though new design paradigms have been introduced, most design practice is still dominated by systematic design procedures, but procedures that are implemented with new tools and new constraints.

Competence and the IBSTPI Competency Development Model

The Nature of Competence and Competencies

With the advent of performance-based educational techniques, competencies have served as the nucleus of program design and development efforts. This movement had various origins. One was the demand for clearly definable measures of program effectiveness in teacher education programs (Dick, Watson and Kaufman, 1981). Competency-based education applied the then innovative systems design techniques and elements of mastery learning (Young and Van Mondfrans, 1972). Competency-based education program design was widely used in both teacher education and K-12 education during the 1970's. These new programs coincided with the work of McClelland (1973) who outlined methods for the identification of competencies that provided non-biased ways of predicting job performance. McClelland's competency approach was applied in organizational human resource functions of employee selection, career pathing, performance appraisal and development. Today, competencies continue to be used in many of these same activities in the business environment.

Nonetheless, there are differing views of the nature of a competency and its relationship to professional competence itself. Parry (1998) cited the tendency for many to mistake competencies for personality traits or characteristics, or for styles and values. Lucia and Lepsinger (1999) see personal characteristics and aptitudes as foundational to skill and knowledge demonstration. It is generally agreed, however, that while competence is the state of being well qualified, competency statements are descriptions of the critical ways in which such competence is demonstrated. Competencies are innately behavioral and positivistic in nature, even though most professionals are fundamentally interested in underlying competence. Spencer and Spencer (1993) portray competency as either core or surface entities, with skills and knowledge being surface variables that are easier to develop than core characteristics such as attitudes.

McLagan (May, 1997) identifies six different approaches to competency definition. She notes that competencies have been viewed as job tasks, as results of work efforts, as outputs, as knowledge, skills and attitudes, as qualities that describe superior performers, and finally, as bundles of attributes.

IBSTPI defines a competency as:

> ...a knowledge, skill, or attitude that enables one to effectively perform the activities of a given occupation or function to the standards expected in employment.

This orientation combines two of the McLagan competency definition models – that of job tasks and of an accumulation of knowledge, skills and attitudes. The IBSTPI competencies are statements of behavior – not personality traits or beliefs, but they do often reflect attitudes. IBSTPI competencies are correlated with performance on a job and are typically measured against commonly accepted standards. Moreover, there is an implication that the IBSTPI competencies can be developed through training. This is consistent with Parry's (1998) interpretation of the general nature of competency statements.

Competencies have been used for many purposes in an organization. Lucia and Lepsinger (1999) describe current manifestations of the functions initiated in the 1970's. These include interviewing prospective employees, hiring qualified persons and facilitating effective performance appraisal and succession planning. In addition, competencies are critical to successful training since they can clarify the necessary job skills, focus the training plans on missing competencies in the work force, and provide a framework for coaching and feedback. Lucia and Lepsinger also site the use of competency models as tools to determine those skills required to meet future needs of the organization. Competencies, such as the IBSTPI ID competencies, can also serve a useful role in academe. They can serve as benchmarking tools for programs and a departure point for course planning and student assessment.

The IBSTPI Generic Competency Development Model

Marrelli (1998) defines a competency model as "the organization of identified competencies into a conceptual framework that enables the people in an organization to understand, talk about, and apply the competencies … an organizing scheme" (p. 10). The generic IBSTPI competency development model is shown in Figure 1.1.

A set of competencies, such as the IBSTPI ID competencies, relates to a job role. The role definition is typically a preliminary step to competency definition. Competencies totally unrelated to actual jobs are typically impossible to use effectively. Job roles, however, can be defined generically or they can be customized to reflect a given work context (Lucia and Lepsinger,

Figure 1.1 The Generic IBSTPI Competency Development Model

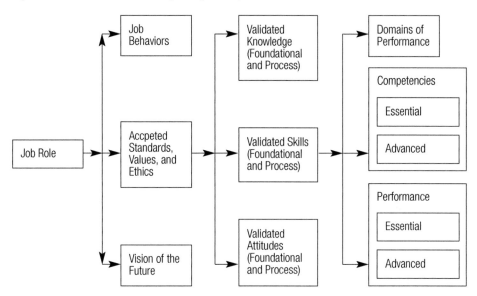

1999). The IBSTPI ID competencies reflect a more generalized view of the designer's job. Consequently, a specific position with a given organization may relate to only a portion of these competencies.

Job roles, however, must be interpreted further to facilitate competency definition. Specific job behaviors must be identified. In addition, the performance and ethical standards and values commonly used in the field to evaluate such behaviors must also be determined. Finally, one must clarify a vision of the field. This vision may be the result of interpretations of current research and emerging trends, or it may be the result of societal or business pressures. Job behaviors, vision, and standards provide the major input into the identification and validation of the knowledge, skills, and attitudes critical to a particular job role.

Structurally, the competency model consists of three components – domains (which in this case primarily follow the design process), competencies, and performance statements. Competency statements in the IBSTPI format are short, general descriptions of complex efforts. One example would be, "Communicate effectively in visual, oral and written form". In this, and all other competencies, additional detail is needed to more fully explain what is entailed in the activity. These explanations are provided via performance statements. A full demonstration of a given competency would then consist of a series of more specific behaviors. For example, the communication competency is partially supported by the performance statement "Deliver presentations that effectively engage and communicate". Competencies and performance statements are structurally the same, differing only in the level of behavior specificity. Performance statements are not, however, simply process descriptions.

Even though competencies are general, they can, nonetheless, be categorized into even larger domains of activity. This competency modeling tactic is recommended by Spencer and Spencer (1993). The IBSTPI design competencies are clustered into domains that, by and large, follow a systematic design approach – planning and analysis, design and development, implementation and management. In addition, there is an initial professional foundations domain. These domains facilitate competency summaries and theme identification, even as the performance statements facilitate detailed analysis. All levels – domain, competency, and performance statement – can be used in program design.

In 1986, the IBSTPI competencies were presented as *core* ID competencies – those that enable a skilled designer to enter an organization and complete the basic instructional systems design process. There was the implicit assumption that these were the fundamental skills of a trained, but novice designer. The updated competencies do not follow this model. Rather, the competencies are comprehensive, encompassing not only those skills, knowledge and attitudes essential for all designers, but those of advanced practitioners as well.

Implementing the Model

The IBSTPI competency development model provides overall direction for the competency development process. In actual operation, there were three major phases used to update the ID competencies, each of which is fundamentally an empirical procedure. The phases are:

- Identification of Foundational Research;
- Competency Drafting; and
- Competency Validation and Rewriting.

Phase I: Foundations. The previous set of IBSTPI competencies, initially based upon an extensive research process, served as the foundation of the current set. In addition, the results of two studies of the competencies of expert instructional designers also served as input. Basic premises and tentative assumptions were articulated and agreed upon. A new base list was developed using these three sources.

Phase II: Competency Drafting. The IBSTPI board of directors served as an expert focus group that analyzed and debated the base list. Competencies and performance statements were rewritten by people with particular expertise in a given area. The new list was analyzed, debated, and rewritten several times to reflect the evolving input and to establish format consistency.

Phase III: Competency Validation and Rewriting. Once a list was established that had full board approval, two survey instruments were devised for general distribution. One instrument focused upon competency and performance statement criticality, and the second on requisite levels of designer expertise. These instruments were administered to instructional design practitioners, academics, and managers in diverse geographical locations and work environments. The final list was modified to reflect the input of this group. When there was a "split decision" situation, the board made the ultimate decision based upon its collective experience and vision.

Assumptions of the IBSTPI ID Competencies

The newly updated designer competencies are based upon ten key assumptions about the nature of instructional design and designers themselves, and the function and role of competencies. These assumptions directed the development process and can also influence one's interpretation of the competencies. They are based not only upon a particular view of the state of the art of design practice, but also upon disciplinary values.

Assumption 1: Instructional designers are those persons who demonstrate design competencies on the job regardless of their job title or training.

Even though most experienced designers take it for granted that it is clear who designers are, in some situations these decisions are not easily made. Certainly many designers have acquired their skills on the job or by attending short workshops, rather than by completing formal academic programs and earning an advanced degree. Likewise, many organizations do not have a formal job title of "instructional designer". For some, the "trainer" is both a designer of instruction as well as a deliverer of instruction. For some, the "performance technologist" assumes instructional design responsibilities. Or perhaps, the "human resource specialist" takes on the instructional design role.

Often designers assume specialized roles. Senior designers, for example, may serve as the project manager, but they are still considered designers even with these expanded responsibilities. Other designers concentrate on only one phase of the process, such as analysis or evaluation. They, too, are still considered to be designers. While it is not unusual for a designer to perform development tasks as well, those who concentrate totally on development or production tasks are *not* considered designers. For example, graphic artists and programmers may be critical members of a design team, but they are not instructional designers.

The IBSTPI competencies pertain to persons whose jobs encompass any portion of the primary design domains. In other words, if one's work pertains to planning and analysis, or design and development, or implementation and management, that person would be considered an instructional designer for these purposes. Whether the designer performs his or her job in a skillful manner is not relevant to one's general classification as a designer. Consequently, these competencies can pertain to a wide variety of persons and jobs.

Assumption 2: ID competencies pertain to persons working in a wide range of job settings.

Not only do practicing designers have many job titles, but also they work in many settings. This phenomenon has occurred as instructional design and training has grown and become more sophisticated over the years. The work environment often shapes design practice. For example, designers working as external consultants frequently have little to do with product implementation or maintenance. At times, they do not even engage in summative evaluation activities. On the other hand, designers working in a given organization (in a sense as internal consultants) are likely to be very involved in program maintenance, in summative evaluation and often impact evaluation. The IBSTPI competencies are applicable to each of these situations.

One point should be highlighted, however. While the IBSTPI ID competencies are not specifically designated as applying only to business applications of instructional design, there is an emphasis on issues and processes more unique to a business environment than those of elementary or secondary education, or of higher education or community-based education. This emphasis reflects where the predominance of design work currently takes place. The business orientation is more obvious in the Implementation and Management domain. Nonetheless, it is not difficult to use the competencies in any setting.

There are vast differences in the resources available from one work setting to another, and these resources often facilitate the demonstration of certain competencies. Their absence from a given work environment, however, does not diminish the validity of the related competency, since the IBSTPI competencies are generalized to the profession at large, transcending the characteristics of a given situation.

Assumption 3: Instructional design is a process most commonly guided by systematic design models and principles.

In the early days of instructional design adherence to a systematic approach to design was typically assumed. Diversity has come with the growth of the field. Today, alternative design paradigms are being used. Visscher-Voerman, Gustafson and Plomp (1999) describe three additional paradigms – communicative, pragmatic, and artistic. The communicative paradigm emphasizes reaching consensus among these parties throughout the design process. The pragmatic approach is distinguished by repeated try-out and revision based upon stakeholders' perceptions. The artistic approach (typical of many technology-based design and development projects) relies on the developer's own subjective criteria, as well as those of clients.

Nonetheless, the IBSTPI competencies are firmly rooted in a belief that the majority of ID practice is still dominated by traditional instructional systems design (ISD) models. These models are exemplified by Dick and Carey (1996), Morrison, Ross and Kemp (2001), Seels and Glasgow (1998), Smith and Ragan, 1999), or by similar models adapted specifically to business and other non-school environments such as Rothwell and Kazanas (1998).

Assumption 4: Instructional design is most commonly seen as resulting in transfer of training and organizational performance improvement.

As the field of instructional design has grown, the prevailing view of the products of design efforts has also changed. Early models simply portrayed the product as an instructional program or material. The more appropriate outcome then was seen as learning, typically in the form of knowledge and skill acquisition. Today the outcome is largely viewed as transfer of training at the least, but to many it is characterized as individual performance improvement and organizational change. This latter view serves as a foundation for the IBSTPI competencies.

It has implications for the competencies and enormous ramifications for the performance statements that more specifically identify the task components. It alters the traditional nature of pre-design analysis and of all phases of evaluation. It profoundly changes one's approach to project management.

The broad performance improvement stance also expands the theoretical foundations of the competencies. The foundational design theory bases now include theories that explain the nature of organizations, human motivation, psychometrics, ergonomics and change (Rosenberg, Coscarelli, and Hutchison, 1999).

Assumption 5: Instructional design competence spans novice, experienced and expert designers.

The 1986 IBSTPI competencies were presented as "core competencies". As such, they summarized the essence of the instructional design process. They were skills that the writers suggested should be possessed by any instructional designer. A comparison of the 1986 and the 2000 competencies would show that this original core still remains. However, the current complexities of the design field are not reflected in the 1986 list.

The current competency updating process started with an agreement among the IBSTPI directors that this list was to be a comprehensive compilation of not only competencies currently viewed as "core", but also of those of expert and more experienced designers. The field now has a rudimentary research foundation that provides a credible definition of design expertise (e.g., see LeMaistre, 1998; Perez and Emery, 1995; Rowland, 1992).

Assumption 6: Few instructional designers, regardless of their levels of expertise, are able to successfully demonstrate all ID competencies.

The very comprehensive nature of the 2000 IBSTPI competencies makes it unlikely that most designers, even those with substantial work experience, will be able to demonstrate each and every competency and performance statement identified. This is consistent with today's instructional design practice that is more complex and more sophisticated than was design practice in the early years of the field. To some extent, this reflects the emergence of areas of design specialization that have evolved, with many design practitioners assuming distinct roles that are directed toward only parts of the design process. In other cases, the apparent specialization is more indicative of the particular emphases that naturally occur in some work environments. Nonetheless, one should not be surprised if all designers can not demonstrate all competencies, or all aspects of a given competency.

Assumption 7: ID competencies are generic and amenable to customization.

The IBSTPI competencies have been constructed so that they speak to generic design issues, and may lack the dominant focus of a particular organization or industry. However, the competencies can be customized to meet the unique characteristics of an organization. Friedlander (1996) suggests that this be accomplished by identifying, documenting and prioritizing those competencies that are important to the success of the organization and then determining how it will measure and assess each competency. Language may also be changed to incorporate terminology unique to the organization or the target industry.

Assumption 8: ID competencies define the manner in which design should be practiced.

Dick, Watson and Kaufman (1981) contrasted two approaches to competency development – a consensus model that emphasized the "what is" and the model-building approach that focused on "what should be". While to a great extent the IBSTPI ID competencies represent a blend of these two approaches, the dominant orientation is the more idealized stance. There was a conscious effort to anticipate the needs of the future, and to establish standards for expert behavior that will advance the field. Consequently, it is possible for some designers to find elements of the new list that are unfamiliar to them. The difficult part of the task was to create competencies that are not only idealistic in nature, but are still practical and useable in actual work environments.

To a great extent the expanding theoretical foundations of instructional design guided this task. The 1986 ID competencies were directed primarily by general systems theory and to a great extent by behavioral learning theory. The updated competencies maintain the systems theory influence, but also reflect cognitive theory and those theory bases associated with performance improvement.

Assumption 9: ID competencies reflect societal and disciplinary values and ethics.

While there was a conscious effort to develop competencies that do not espouse disciplinary biases, competencies are nonetheless influenced by the context in which they were devised. They are shaped not only by the forces operating within a field, but also by the larger context in which one works. The values of society at large impact competency construction. For example, there is a current societal emphasis on cultural diversity and accommodating to persons with a wide range of backgrounds and abilities. Not surprisingly, this force influenced the wording of the new IBSTPI ID competencies. The incorporation of societal values is not seen as a deficiency, but rather as one way in which a list of competencies serves as an expression of ideal behavior – the standards to which we should aspire.

Assumption 10: ID competencies should be meaningful and useful to designers worldwide.

Given that instructional design is now a global activity, there was a conscious effort to construct the new ID competencies in such a way that they were applicable to designers working in many countries and many cultures. This has been done by attempting to make each competency and performance statement culture-free. Terminology was changed to remove language unique to the United State's design environment. The validation process included design practitioners working in the major markets throughout the world.

An Overview of the ID Competency Discussion

The remainder of this book is a detailed examination of the new competencies themselves. The basic list is presented in Chapter 2 and they are discussed and put into a workplace context in Chapter 3. This chapter explores the dimensions and implications of each competency and its supporting performance statements. Chapter 4 consists of an examination of the various ways in which the competencies can be used by designers working in a variety of situations. It also includes a discussion of the issues surrounding the certification of designers. Chapter 5 examines the ID competencies as they relate to key ID specializations – the analyst/evaluator, the E-learning specialist, and the project manager.

Part II of this book provides a report of the competency validation study. The data that served as the basis for developing and finalizing the competencies and performance statements are presented and discussed. These data establish the underlying integrity of the IBSTPI ID competencies. This section may appeal only to those interested in ID research. Finally, the Epilogue briefly discusses future IBSTPI efforts in competency development pertinent to instructional design and related areas.

The appendices present additional documents that can facilitate one's understanding and use of the new IBSTPI ID competencies. The new IBSTPI Code of Ethical Standards is presented here, as well as a glossary of terms and references for further study of the ID process. These materials may be useful to those wishing to expand their knowledge of instructional design and its applicability to their work.

Chapter 2

The 2000 IBSTPI Instructional Design Competencies[*]

There are 23 newly updated IBSTPI instructional design competencies. These competencies are clustered into four general domains and are supported by 122 performance statements. The domain groupings serve organizational and conceptual functions, and they also suggest the scope and inter-relatedness of instructional designers' job tasks.

In each of the four domains there are specific skills and knowledge which every instructional designer is expected to master (labeled as "essential"), as well as skills and knowledge that only the most experienced and expert designers would be expected to master (labeled as "advanced"). These domains reflect the fact that the field of instructional design has grown in breadth, depth, and complexity such that no one person can be expected to master all related skills and knowledge.

The entire list of competencies and performance statements is presented in the remainder of this chapter. In addition, there are supporting documents in the Appendix that may aid in their interpretation. First, the glossary of instructional design terms in Appendix B provides definitions of key words used here and throughout this book. The bibliography of instructional design references, in Appendix C, lists books, chapters and articles that provide further discussion and explanation of the design topics raised in the competency list. These references are grouped in terms of:

- General ID books;
- ID research and theory;
- ID models, tools, and techniques;
- Professional Foundations;
- Planning and Analysis
- Multimedia and E-learning;
- Evaluation;
- Implementation and Management; and
- Journals.

The ID Domains, Competencies and Performance Statements: 2000 Version

PROFESSIONAL FOUNDATIONS

1 *Communicate effectively in visual, oral and written form.* (Essential)
   a) Create messages that accommodate learner needs and characteristics, content, and objectives. (Essential)
   b) Write and edit text to produce messages that are clear, concise, and grammatically correct. (Essential)
   c) Apply principles of message design to page layout and screen design. (Essential)

d) Create or select visuals that instruct, orient, or motivate. (Essential)

e) Deliver presentations that effectively engage and communicate. (Essential)

f) Use active listening skills in all situations. (Essential)

g) Present and receive information in a manner that is appropriate for the norms and tasks of the group or team. (Essential)

h) Seek and share information and ideas among individuals with diverse backgrounds and roles. (Essential)

i) Facilitate meetings effectively. (Essential)

2   Apply current research and theory to the practice of instructional design. (Advanced)

a) Promote, apply and disseminate the results of instructional design theory and research. (Advanced)

b) Read instructional design research, theory and practice literature. (Essential)

c) Apply concepts, techniques and theory of other disciplines to problems of learning, instruction and instructional design. (Advanced)

3   Update and improve one's knowledge, skills and attitudes pertaining to instructional design and related fields. (Essential)

a) Apply developments in instructional design and related fields. (Advanced)

b) Acquire and apply new technology skills to instructional design practice. (Essential)

c) Participate in professional activities. (Essential)

d) Document one's work as a foundation for future efforts, publications or professional presentation. (Advanced)

e) Establish and maintain contacts with other professionals. (Essential)

4   Apply fundamental research skills to instructional design projects. (Advanced)

a) Use a variety of data collection tools and procedures. (Advanced)

b) Apply appropriate research and methodologies to needs assessment and evaluation. (Advanced)

c) Use basic statistical techniques in needs assessment and evaluation. (Advanced)

d) Write research and evaluation reports. (Advanced)

5 *Identify and resolve ethical and legal implications of design in the work place.* (Advanced)

a) Identify ethical and legal dimensions of instructional design practice. (Advanced)

b) Anticipate and respond to ethical consequences of design decisions. (Advanced)

c) Recognize and respect intellectual property rights of others. (Essential)

d) Recognize the ethical and legal implications and consequences of instructional products. (Advanced)

e) Adhere to regulatory guidelines and organizational policies. (Essential)

PLANNING AND ANALYSIS

6 *Conduct a needs assessment.* (Essential)

a) Describe the problem and its dimensions, identifying the discrepancies between current and desired performance. (Essential)

b) Clarify the varying perceptions of need and their implications. (Advanced)

c) Select and use appropriate needs assessment tools and techniques. (Essential)

d) Determine the possible causes of the problem and potential solutions. (Essential)

e) Recommend and advocate non-instructional solutions when appropriate. (Advanced)

f) Complete a cost benefit analysis for recommended solutions. (Advanced)

7 *Design a curriculum or program.* (Essential)
   a) Determine the scope of the curriculum or program. (Essential)
   b) Specify courses based upon needs assessment outcomes. (Essential)
   c) Sequence courses for learners and groups of learners. (Essential)
   d) Analyze and modify existing curricula or programs to insure adequate content coverage. (Essential)
   e) Modify an existing curriculum or program to reflect changes in society, the knowledge base, technology, or the organization. (Advanced)

8 *Select and use a variety of techniques for determining instructional content.* (Essential)
   a) Identify content requirements in accordance with needs assessment findings. (Essential)
   b) Elicit, synthesize and validate content from subject matter experts and other sources. (Advanced)
   c) Determine the breadth and depth of intended content coverage given instructional constraints. (Advanced)
   d) Determine prerequisites given the type of subject matter, the needs of the learners and the organization. (Essential)
   e) Use appropriate techniques to analyze varying types of content. (Essential)

9 *Identify and describe target population characteristics.* (Essential)
   a) Determine characteristics of the target population influencing learning and transfer. (Essential)
   b) Analyze, evaluate and select learner profile data for use in a particular design situation. (Advanced)

10 *Analyze the characteristics of the environment.* (Essential)
   a) Identify aspects of the physical and social environments that impact the delivery of instruction. (Essential)
   b) Identify environmental and cultural aspects that influence attitudes toward instructional interventions. (Advanced)
   c) Identify environmental and cultural factors that influence learning, attitudes, and performance. (Advanced)
   d) Identify the nature and role of varying work environments in the teaching and learning processes. (Advanced)
   e) Determine the extent to which organizational mission, philosophy and values influence the design and success of a project. (Advanced)

11 *Analyze the characteristics of existing and emerging technologies and their use in an instructional environment.* (Essential)
   a) Specify the capabilities of existing and emerging technologies to enhance motivation, visualization, interaction, simulation, and individualization. (Essential)
   b) Evaluate the capacity of a given infrastructure to support selected technologies. (Advanced)
   c) Assess the benefits of existing and emerging technologies. (Essential)

12 *Reflect upon the elements of a situation before finalizing design solutions and strategies.* (Essential)
   a) Generate multiple solutions to a given problem situation. (Advanced)
   b) Remain open to alternative solutions until sufficient data have been collected and verified. (Essential)
   c) Assess the consequences and implications of design decisions on the basis of prior experience, intuition and knowledge. (Advanced)
   d) Revisit selected solutions continuously and adjust as necessary. (Advanced)

DESIGN AND DEVELOPMENT

13 Select, modify, or create a design and development model appropriate for a given project. (Advanced)
   a) Consider multiple design and development models. (Advanced)
   b) Select or create a model suitable for the project based on an analysis of model elements. (Advanced)
   c) Modify the model if project parameters change. (Advanced)
   d) Provide a rationale for the selected design and development model. (Advanced)

14 Select and use a variety of techniques to define and sequence the instructional content and strategies. (Essential)
   a) Use appropriate techniques to identify the conditions that determine the scope of the instructional content. (Essential)
   b) Use appropriate techniques to specify and sequence instructional goals and objectives. (Essential)
   c) Select appropriate media and delivery systems. (Essential)
   d) Analyze the learning outcomes and select appropriate strategies. (Essential)
   e) Analyze the instructional context and select appropriate strategies. (Essential)
   f) Select appropriate participation and motivational strategies. (Essential)
   g) Select and sequence assessment techniques. (Essential)
   h) Prepare a design document and circulate for review and approval. (Essential)

15 Select or modify existing instructional materials. (Essential)
   a) Identify existing instructional materials for reuse or modification consistent with instructional specifications. (Essential)
   b) Select materials to support the content analyses, proposed technologies, delivery methods and instructional strategies. (Essential)

c) Use cost-benefit analyses to decide whether to modify, purchase or develop instructional materials. (Advanced)

d) Work with subject matter experts to validate material selection or modification. (Essential)

e) Integrate existing instructional materials into the design. (Essential)

16 *Develop instructional materials.* (Essential)

a) Develop materials that support the content analyses, proposed technologies, delivery methods and instructional strategies. (Essential)

b) Work with subject matter experts during the development process. (Essential)

c) Produce instructional materials in a variety of delivery formats. (Essential)

17 *Design instruction that reflects an understanding of the diversity of learners and groups of learners.* (Essential)

a) Design instruction that accommodates different learning styles. (Essential)

b) Be sensitive to the cultural impact of instructional materials. (Essential)

c) Accommodate cultural factors that may influence learning in the design. (Essential)

18 *Evaluate and assess instruction and its impact.* (Essential)

a) Construct reliable and valid test items using a variety of formats. (Advanced)

b) Identify the processes and outcomes to be measured given the identified problem and proposed solutions. (Essential)

c) Develop and implement formative evaluation plans. (Essential)

d) Develop and implement summative evaluation plans. (Essential)

e) Develop and implement confirmative evaluation plans. (Advanced)

f) Determine the impact of instruction on the organization. (Advanced)

g) Identify and assess the sources of evaluation data. (Essential)

h) Manage the evaluation process. (Advanced)

i) Discuss and interpret evaluation reports with stakeholders. (Advanced)

IMPLEMENTATION AND MANAGEMENT

19 *Plan and manage instructional design projects. (Advanced)*

a) Establish project scope and goals. (Advanced)

b) Use a variety of techniques and tools to develop a project plan. (Advanced)

c) Write project proposals. (Advanced)

d) Develop project information systems. (Advanced)

e) Monitor multiple instructional design projects. (Advanced)

f) Allocate resources to support the project plan. (Advanced)

g) Select and manage internal and external consultants. (Advanced)

h) Monitor congruence between performance and project plans. (Advanced)

i) Troubleshoot project problems. (Advanced)

j) Debrief design team to establish lessons learned. (Advanced)

20 *Promote collaboration, partnerships and relationships among the participants in a design project.* (Advanced)

a) Identify how and when collaboration and partnerships should be promoted. (Advanced)

b) Identify stakeholders and the nature of their involvement. (Advanced)

c) Identify subject matter experts to participate in the design and development process. (Advanced)

d) Build and promote effective relationships that may impact a design project. (Advanced)

e) Determine how to use cross functional teams. (Advanced)

f) Promote and manage the interactions among team members. (Advanced)

g) Plan for the diffusion of instructional or performance improvement products. (Advanced)

21 *Apply business skills to managing instructional design.* (Advanced)

a) Link design efforts to strategic plans of the organization. (Advanced)

b) Establish strategic and tactical goals for the design function. (Advanced)

c) Use a variety of techniques to establish standards of excellence. (Advanced)

d) Develop a business case to promote the critical role of the design function. (Advanced)

e) Recruit, retain, and develop instructional design personnel. (Advanced)

f) Provide financial plans and controls for the instructional design function. (Advanced)

g) Maintain management and stakeholder support of the design function. (Advanced)

h) Market services and manage customer relations. (Advanced)

22 *Design instructional management systems.* (Advanced)

a) Establish systems for documenting learner progress and course completion. (Advanced)

b) Establish systems for maintaining records and issuing reports of individual and group progress. (Advanced)

c) Establish systems for diagnosing individual needs and prescribing instructional alternatives. (Advanced)

23 Provide for the effective implementation of instructional products and programs. (Essential)

- a) Use evaluation data as a guide for revision of products and programs. (Advanced)
- b) Update instructional products and programs as required. (Essential)
- c) Monitor and revise the instructional delivery process as required. (Essential)
- d) Revise instructional products and programs to reflect changes in professional practice or policy. (Essential)
- e) Revise instructional products and programs to reflect changes in the organization or the target population. (Essential)
- f) Recommend plans for organizational support of instructional programs. (Advanced)

Chapter 3

The ID Competencies: Discussion and Analysis

With Timothy W. Spannaus and J. Michael Spector

The substantially extended content in the updated IBSTPI ID competencies reflects the current complexity of instructional design praxis (see, for example, Tennyson, Schott, Seel and Dijkstra, 1997). The following discussions present a rationale and explanation of this new list, especially that which is novel and broadened. The rationale and perspective presented here reflects the prevalent and prominent views of the international instructional design community. These four domains and their components present an integrated account of what instructional design professionals can reasonably be expected to know and do at this point in time.

Professional Foundations

The first competency domain is Professional Foundations, and it pertains to five competency areas:

- Effective communication;
- Application of research and theory;
- Updating and improving one's skills;
- Using research skills; and,
- Ethical and legal dimensions of design.

This competency domain is an explicit recognition of the current professional status of the instructional design field. The bulk of this domain is completely new. As with any profession, this status has associated obligations and expectations. These obligations and expectations range from clear and coherent communication skills to responsibilities for advancing the profession and advancing within the profession. Each competency will be discussed.

Competency 1: Communicate effectively in visual, oral and written form. (Essential). There are nine component performance areas supporting this competency, including:

> *a) Create messages that accommodate learner needs and characteristics, content, and objectives. (Essential)*
>
> *b) Write and edit text to produce messages that are clear, concise, and grammatically correct. (Essential)*
>
> *c) Apply principles of message design to page layout and screen design. (Essential)*
>
> *d) Create or select visuals that instruct, orient, or motivate. (Essential Core)*
>
> *e) Deliver presentations that effectively engage and communicate. (Essential)*
>
> *f) Use active listening skills in all situations. (Essential)*

g) Present and receive information in a manner that is appropriate for the norms and tasks of the group or team. (Essential)

h) Seek and share information and ideas among individuals with diverse backgrounds and roles. (Essential)

i) Facilitate meetings effectively. (Essential)

The role of effective communications is emphasized in this set of standards even more than in the 1986 set. This reflects the perspective that instructional design practice today is essentially a multi-disciplinary, multi-person, and often multi-organizational activity. As a consequence, effective communications skills are vital. The foundational research supporting this competency was perhaps most consistent, and insistent, in affirming that that this particular competency was indeed essential for all instructional designers.

Communication skills are an essential and foundational aspect of being an instructional designer, and each related performance statement is considered essential. Effective communication is vital to the success of nearly all instructional design projects. As a consequence, every instructional designer should be able to write clear and easily understood text, to create or select effective supporting visual representations, and to facilitate meetings. They create messages for targeted learners, determine page and screen layouts, and make formal presentations.

Instructional design is not a solitary activity and designers must work effectively in group settings, often in a position of leadership. Typically, instructional designers organize meetings with clients, sponsors, other project groups and instructional design team members to discuss and explain various aspects of an instructional design project. Those with whom instructional designers typically interact often come from different disciplines, have different backgrounds, and represent different roles within a project or organization. Understanding group dynamics and being aware of group expectations is essential for effective teamwork.

Competency 2: Apply current research and theory to the practice of instructional design. (Advanced). The components of this competency are:
   a) Promote, apply and disseminate the results of instructional design theory and research. (Advanced)
   b) Read instructional design research, theory and practice literature. (Essential)
   c) Apply concepts, techniques and theory of other disciplines to problems of learning, instruction and instructional design. (Advanced)

There is an identifiable literature reflecting instructional design theory, research, development, and practice. As practitioners advance in their design careers, they should become familiar with much of that literature, as well as the research literature from other fields related to instructional design (see, for example, De Corte and Weinert, 1996). Most importantly, they should be able to apply it to solve practical instructional design problems.

Even novice designers are expected to read relevant research and professional literature. Expert practitioners, on the other hand, are expected to effectively integrate relevant educational research findings into their work, as well as actively contribute to instructional design theory and research. Being a recognized expert practitioner implies regularly explaining such research to others. In short, this competency and its performance statements recognizes that there is an instructional design community, and being an expert practitioner implies active participation in that community.

Competency 3: Update and improve one's knowledge, skills and attitudes pertaining to instructional design and related fields. (Essential) There are five performance components, including:
   a) Apply developments in instructional design and related fields. (Advanced)
   b) Acquire and apply new technology skills to instructional design practice. (Essential)
   c) Participate in professional activities. (Essential)

d) Document one's work as a foundation for future efforts, publications or professional presentation. (Advanced)

e) Establish and maintain contacts with other professionals. (Essential)

Every instructional designer is expected to engage in ongoing efforts to update and improve his or her ID knowledge and skills. Instructional design is related to such fields as cognitive science, human factors, psychology of learning, and organizational psychology. Consequently, instructional design experts should be familiar with developments in such fields, as well as with current research and thinking in the area of instructional design. This would include, for example, keeping abreast of basic research relating to human perception, cognitive processing and memory. Designers must also maintain currency with applied research, such as that pertaining to multimedia design or distributed learning environments. They should feel comfortable with reading both qualitative and quantitative methods, ranging from case studies investigations to controlled experimental designs.

In addition to keeping up with the literature, expert practitioners are expected to document their work as a basis for future projects, as well as for presentation and publication in professional venues. Such documentation is critical to advancing the field. However, it is important for professionals to advance themselves as well. One way is to maintain contact with other practitioners and to participate regularly in professional activities.

A special aspect of knowledge updating critical to instructional designers relates to new technologies. This involves learning about technologies and their use in expediting design tasks, as well as how they might be integrated into design projects to support knowledge acquisition and transfer.

Competency 4: Apply fundamental research skills to instructional design projects. (Advanced) There are four performance statements related to this competency – all of which are advanced skills. They are:

  a) Use a variety of data collection tools and procedures. (Advanced)

  b) Apply appropriate research and methodologies to needs assessment and evaluation. (Advanced)

  c) Use basic statistical techniques in needs assessment and evaluation. (Advanced)

  d) Write research and evaluation reports. (Advanced)

Good designers typically use research strategies. The ability to apply fundamental research skills to instructional design, however, is considered an advanced skill, and all of the associated performance statements are also categorized as advanced. These skills characterize expert designers.

Fundamental research skills involve a variety of abilities, including: determining which methods are appropriate for particular research problems and questions; designing appropriate research studies and experiments, especially for evaluation purposes; developing appropriate research instruments and tools (for example, questionnaires and interview protocols); and, analyzing, interpreting and synthesizing research findings. Instructional design research most often is based on a particular instructional design model, and may even involve an investigation of the adequacy of that model. Instructional design research is conducted on all aspects of the process, including needs analysis, curriculum planning, and evaluation.

Areas of investigation currently of keen interest to instructional design researchers include topics such as: cognitive task analysis, efficacy of design models, efficiency of design practices and tools, learning effectiveness measures, summative evaluation techniques, technology-based learning and user-centered formative evaluation methods. Expert practitioners must develop and maintain the requisite knowledge and skills to apply research findings, and hopefully some designer practitioners will also contribute to this body of research as well.

Competency 5: Identify and resolve ethical and legal implications of design in the work place. (Advanced) Five aspects of ethical and legal competence have been identified, including:

    a) Identify ethical and legal dimensions of instructional design practice. (Advanced)

    b) Anticipate and respond to ethical consequences of design decisions. (Advanced)

    c) Recognize and respect intellectual property rights of others. (Essential)

    d) Recognize the ethical and legal implications and consequences of instructional products. (Advanced)

    e) Adhere to regulatory guidelines and organizational policies. (Essential)

As with any type of professional practice, there are ethical and legal obligations for practitioners. This set of standards makes these obligations explicit for instructional designers, and it is the first to recognize ethical and legal obligations explicitly. The need for this competency became obvious in discussions of intellectual property right issues with regard to web-based instructional materials. This is currently an area of great concern because of the ease with which such rights can now be violated.

In addition to formal legal codes and codes of ethics, many organizations have standard operating procedures, guidelines, and/or policies. Many of these impact the practice of instructional design. Typically, instructional designers are expected to follow such guidelines and explain or justify any deviations. As instructional designers advance in the profession, they often become project leaders. In these roles, designer responsibilities expand and these new positions often demand the ability to anticipate and, when possible, to avoid undesirable ethical conflicts and situations. All expert practitioners are expected to be able to identify the ethical and legal dimensions associated with the practice of instructional design. However, novices must be aware of regulatory guidelines and respect intellectual property rights.

IBSTPI has identified specific ethical standards pertinent to the work of instructional designers. These standards provide further explanation of the nature of ethical designer behavior. They are found in Appendix D. These standards relate to four general areas of ethics: Responsibilities to Others, Social Mandates, Respecting the Rights of Others, and Professional Practice.

Planning and Analysis

While the Professional Foundations competencies establish ID as a profession, the seven competencies in the Planning and Analysis domain describe some of the most basic skills of this profession. Many designers see their strongest attributes as their ability to systematically analyze a problem or situation and move toward a solution. There are seven competencies in the domain of planning and analysis, and thirty performance statements. These competencies represent critical components in the ID process. It is in this phase that the foundational data for the project is collected in the needs assessment, the general design of the program is determined, content is validated, the learners and the learning environment are analyzed, and technology use is determined.

All of the competencies in this domain are essential. Therefore, all competent designers should be able to demonstrate these knowledge, skills and attitudes. The seven competencies in the Planning and Analysis domain relate to:

- Needs assessment;
- Curriculum or program design;
- Determining instructional content;
- Target population characteristics;
- Environmental analysis;

- Using emerging technologies; and
- Reflection.

Typically, the performance of planning and analysis tasks requires interactions with subject matter experts (SME's) since this is the stage in which the designer defines the content that will serve as the foundation of the final product. The discussion of competencies six through twelve and their accompanying performance statements follows.

Competency 6. Conduct a needs assessment. (Essential) There are six performances related to needs assessment, including:

a) *Describe the problem and its dimensions, identifying the discrepancies between current and desired performance. (Essential)*

b) *Clarify the varying perceptions of need and their implications. (Advanced)*

c) *Select and use appropriate needs assessment tools and techniques. (Essential)*

d) *Determine the possible causes of the problem and potential solutions. (Essential)*

e) *Recommend and advocate non-instructional solutions when appropriate. (Advanced)*

f) *Complete a cost benefit analysis for recommended solutions. (Advanced)*

The mixture of essential and advanced skills required in this competency is indicative of the complex nature of needs assessment. The three performance statements requiring advanced skill and knowledge are those where solutions are called for, and judgments and recommendations are made. In each case, poor decisions can have serious consequences for the final product. Their demonstration requires a high level of design expertise.

Needs assessment essentially responds to three questions – Where are we now? Where are we going? and How will we get there? It is a process of examining the perceived gap between an existing situation and those circumstances to which an organization aspires. It is a process that should result in identifying solutions to an organization's problems.

The complexity of most organizations today require designers to conduct a correspondingly complex needs assessment often addressing not only content dimensions, but the nature of the learners and the culture of the organization as well. Designer success is increasingly as dependent on being sensitive to the social morays and culture of an organization as on a knowledge of needs assessment tools and techniques. This is requisite to accurate identification and interpretation of organizational problems, and it is required in most circumstances to creatively select solutions to such problems.

Instructional designers are routinely expected to be able to differentiate between the need for instructional and non-instructional interventions, and select the most cost effective alternative. Today it is critical that instructional designers be as familiar with non-instructional solutions and interventions as they are with traditional instructional solutions, since their goal is ultimately to improve on-the-job performance and solve organizational problems.

Competency 7. Design a curriculum or program. (Essential) The componenys are:
- *a) Determine the scope of the curriculum or program. (Essential)*
- *a) Specify courses based upon needs assessment outcomes. (Essential)*
- *a) Sequence courses for learners and groups of learners. (Essential)*
- *a) Analyze and modify existing curricula or programs to insure adequate content coverage. (Essential)*
- *a) Modify an existing curriculum or program to reflect changes in society, the knowledge base, technology, or the organization. (Advanced)*

In addition to designing instructional products, designers also create entire curricula. Such efforts may be directed toward building new programs or modifying those that currently exist. While the notion of "curriculum" has more commonly been associated with elementary and secondary education, curricula in business environments are now prevalent. Curricula may encompass a series of courses related to a given subject matter crucial to the organization. However, curricula may also pertain to instruction that facilitates an individual's advancement along a particular career path.

In either case, designers contend with large blocks of content, but still employ the fundamental design skills. Programs are based on needs assessment and learner data. Scope and sequence decisions are required, but here they are made in reference to courses and content rather than learning activities and more specific objectives.

The skills related to these curriculum and program design efforts are, for the most part, considered essential. Only one performance is considered advanced. Curriculum modifications made to accommodate societal changes, or changes in the organization, the discipline or even in technology requires more sophisticated skills, according to those who validated these competencies.

Competency 8. Select and use a variety of techniques for determining instructional content. (Essential) This competency consists of the following five component performances:

   a) *Identify content requirements in accordance with needs assessment findings (Essential)*
   b) *Elicit, synthesize and validate content from subject matter experts and other sources. (Advanced)*
   c) *Determine the breadth and depth of the intended content coverage given instructional constraints. (Advanced)*
   d) *Determine prerequisites given the type of subject matter, the needs of the learners and the organization. (Essential)*
   e) *Use appropriate techniques to analyze varying types of content. (Essential)*

This competency is focused upon content identification, a critical aspect of planning and analysis. It is a process that is essential for each design project. Consequently, basic skills in content identification are essential to all designers. Content must reflect needs assessment data, be classified as instructional or prerequisite, and be specified in a manner that is appropriate for the skill level and background of expected learners. There are a variety of techniques that can be used for content identification, and novice designers must have some familiarity with them.

Content identification can be complex. It may involve extensive work with experts in subjects quite unknown to the designer. This demands advanced skills, and experience, in questioning and drawing information out of persons who may have difficulty describing what they know well in terms that the uninitiated can understand. Content identification can also involve eliminating the "nice to know" information so that the instruction may highlight the "need to know" content. This is typically a process of very precisely analyzing and understanding organizational and learner needs so that content truly unnecessary can be eliminated. These advanced content identification skills require designers to engage in high level cognitive processing. They often involve detailed analysis, complex synthesis, and validating one's conclusions.

Competency 9. Identify and describe target population characteristics. (Essential)
There are two components to this competency. They are:
   a) Determine characteristics of the target population influencing learning and transfer. (Essential)
   b) Analyze, evaluate and select learner profile data for use in a particular design situation. (Advanced)

Most trainee groups today are more diverse than was typical in the past. There are ranges of cultural and educational backgrounds, and age. There are ranges of expectations and work pressures. Implementing instructional designs on a global basis only exacerbates these conditions, and yet today, the field knows all too well that quality designs must accommodate such factors. No longer is it only important to be cognizant of the learners' prerequisite skills when designers and trainers are being held accountable for organizational performance improvement.

Learner analysis skills are deceptively complex, and yet extremely important to both the short and long-term success of any design project. When identifying the characteristics of the audience, designers are confronted with a unique challenge. They must determine not only what the characteristics of the targeted learners are, but they must know which of these are critical to the success of the instruction and which characteristics impact learning. It is even more difficult to select those characteristics that influence transfer. So, even though all designers, even beginners, must be able to gather learner data, it is typically up to the advanced designers to work with such data and decide what is critical to a given project.

Competency 10. Analyze the characteristics of the environment. (Essential) The five components of this competency are:
  a) Identify aspects of the physical and social environments that impact the delivery of instruction. (Essential)
  b) Identify environmental and cultural aspects that influence attitudes toward instructional interventions (Advanced)
  c) Identify environmental and cultural factors that influence learning, attitudes and performance. (Advanced)
  d) Identify the nature and role of varying work environments in the teaching and learning process. (Advanced)
  e) Determine the extent to which organizational mission, philosophy and values influence the design and success of a project. (Advanced)

This competency and its supporting performance statements speak to role of the organization in successful training. It speaks to the importance of an organization's physical dimensions and its culture. When instructional design is oriented towards performance improvement (rather than knowledge acquisition), the issues raised by this competency become critical.

Successful designers have long recognized the importance of careful analysis of both the physical and social aspects of the instructional environment, and the cost of neglecting them. Factors such as lighting, air conditioning and heat, equipment, and refreshments all contribute to training success. However, disciplinary research has also verified other environmental conditions that are critical to the ID process. An organization's culture, mission, vision, and values all influence training success. The degree of supervisory and co-worker support, for example, exerts great influence on the extent to which newly acquired knowledge and skills are transferred to the workplace.

Performance improvement interventions are typically ineffective when the organization has not been thoroughly and accurately analyzed, and the data from such analyses have not been factored into the design and delivery of the instruction. While novice designers should be able to deal with the physical dimensions of the instructional environment, experts have a much higher probability of success when dealing with organizational climate factors. As with the complexities of incorporating learner data into designs, it seems to take an expert to address the psychological aspects of a work climate in a training design.

Competency 11. Analyze the characteristics of existing and emerging technologies and their use in an instructional environment. (Essential) The three performance components of this competency are:

  a) *Specify the capabilities of existing and emerging technologies to enhance motivation, visualization, interaction, simulation, and individualization. (Essential)*

  b) *Evaluate the capacity of a given infrastructure to support selected technologies. (Advanced)*

  c) *Assess the benefits of existing and emerging technologies. (Essential)*

One of the most obvious differences between the work of an instructional designer in 1986 when the first IBSTPI designer competencies were published and now is the role of technology. Even though computers were used in the design and delivery of instruction in 1986, the role of technology was far more limited than it is today. This competency and its supporting performance statements reflects these advancements and the fact that it is now almost universally expected that designers have substantial proficiency in technology.

All designers should have knowledge of the uses and benefits of technology in instructional situations. While they may not be skilled HTML programmers or video producers, for example, they should be able to select those technologies that would enhance a given design and provide technicians with the specifications for development. In many respects, this is the modern form of media selection.

Designers should also use technology to facilitate individualization of instruction, to motivate learners, to build creative and engaging approaches to instruction. Designers should be able to use technology to simulate and authentically present complex problem and decision-making situations. Designers are expected to use technology to facilitate learner involvement, even when instructors and content experts are separated by time or distance from the learners. Designers should also know the limitations of technology and when it is not a cost-effective delivery solution.

Some designers are more knowledgeable than others with respect to technology. Often these advanced designers go beyond merely creating instructional products and programs; they create the infrastructure that facilitates the use of technology in instruction. Networked environments, for example, provide opportunities for distance learning, just-in-time training, and knowledge management.

Competency 12. Reflect upon the elements of a situation before finalizing design solutions and strategies. (Essential) This competency has four component performance statements. They are:

   a) Generate multiple solutions to a given problem situation. (Advanced)

   b) Remain open to alternative solutions until sufficient data have been collected and verified. (Essential)

   c) Access the consequences and implications of design decisions on the basis of prior experience, intuition and knowledge. (Advanced)

   d) Revisit selected solutions continuously and adjust as necessary. (Advanced)

Rowland (1993) empirically supported the view of expert designers as persons who reflected upon their work. Analysis, then, is not simply a pre-design activity, but an on-going thinking activity throughout the design process when completed by experts. Those designers who participated in the validation of these competencies, however, perceived generalized reflection as an essential element of successful design for all designers, novice and expert.

Reflection is commonly associated with professional work, and it is specifically associated with professional educators (Peterson, 1995; Schön, 1983). Reflective designers are not simply contemplative, but are measured in their practice. This caution tends to occur during the planning and analysis phases. It includes an avoidance of resolving design problems and identify design solutions any earlier than absolutely necessary. This is not simply a delaying tactic. Instead more experienced designers know that needs assessment data often needs to be verified before it can be assumed to be reliable. Experienced designers know that solutions initially conceived, while perhaps seeming obvious, are often not the best; they are not likely to be the most creative. Experienced designers know that design solutions often need to be revisited and modified as the underlying complexities of an organizational problem become more clear. This all characterizes design reflection.

At times, expert instructional designers act in a seemingly intuitive manner. In fact, such behavior typically involves acting upon the basis of past experiences and recognizing similarities among design problems. This experience allows a designer to understand the intricacies of a given problem and anticipate the consequences of particular design solutions. This, too, is reflection.

The fundamental aspects of reflection are remaining open to alternative solutions and thinking about these options before making a final decision. This is an essential skill of all designers. Only advanced designers, however, typically can generate the various solutions, assess them fully, and then know when to change them.

Design and Development

It is not a surprise that instructional designers are expected to be able to design and develop instructional materials. However, as the discipline expands and as new technologies and methods are introduced, these basic activities become more challenging and more sophisticated. Nonetheless, at first glance the Design and Development competencies appear quite similar to the 1986 ID competencies. Even though many basic design and development tasks remain fundamentally the same, new technologies have led to new ID methodologies. These new technologies are in large part responsible for the significant expansion of the field. This domain pertains to six competency areas:

- Design and development models;
- Sequencing content and strategies;
- Selecting or modifying materials;
- Development;
- Learner diversity; and
- Evaluation and assessment.

These are essential skills of all instructional designers, and the instructional design community remains just as convinced in year 2000 as it was in 1986 that sound design and development are critical to successful instruction.

Competency 13.   Select, modify, or create a design and development model appropriate for a given project. (Advanced) There are four key component performances related to this competency. They are:
   a) Consider multiple design and development models. (Advanced)
   b) Select or create a model suitable for the project based on an analysis of model elements. (Advanced)
   c) Modify the model if project parameters change. (Advanced)
   d) Provide a rationale for the selected design and development model. (Advanced)

This is the only competency in the Design and Development domain that is characteristic of expert instructional designers, and each of its related performance statements is also considered to be advanced. This competency is new to this 2000 version. Expert designers often make novel contributions in the form of new instructional design and development models, often by customizing generic models to a particular work setting or to key project variables. They may make significant alterations to existing models. In addition, they are able to justify to others why they have selected, modified, or created this new model. In that sense they are marketing ID and educating others.

In most graduate programs that prepare instructional designers, students are taught a given design model. They are encouraged to use that model as a guide in their subsequent design work. Some new graduates are dismayed at the seeming lack of attention being paid to traditional ID models in the "real world" of work. In fact, many experienced designers are constantly adapting these procedures (or selecting from a variety of alternative design models) to accommodate the idiosyncrasies of a particular project, particular clients, or particular organizations. If done well, this facility to adjust models to project demands lays the foundation for project success.

Competency 14. Select and use a variety of techniques to define and sequence the instructional content and strategies. (Essential) There are eight performance statements associated with this competency, and all eight represent skills and knowledge that are essential for all instructional designers. They are:

   a) Use appropriate techniques to identify the conditions that determine the scope of the instructional content. (Essential)

   b) Use appropriate techniques to specify and sequence instructional goals and objectives. (Essential)

   c) Select appropriate media and delivery systems. (Essential)

   d) Analyze the learning outcomes and select appropriate strategies. (Essential)

   e) Analyze the instructional context and select appropriate strategies. (Essential)

   f) Select appropriate participation and motivational strategies. (Essential)

   g) Select and sequence assessment techniques. (Essential)

   h) Prepare a design document and circulate for review and approval. (Essential)

Regardless of the particular technologies or the project thrust, designers must always engage in strategy selection and sequencing. This process often involves frequent interaction with content specialists – the subject matter experts. Maintaining close contact with these persons is becoming recognized as a crucial activity for instructional designers, as shown by the increasing interest in and emphasis on participatory and user-centered design (see, for example, Carr-Chellman, Cuyar and Breman, 1998; Koshmann 1996).

However, strategy selection and sequencing is a complex cluster of tasks that first depend upon determining the scope of the design effort – the range and order of the content goals and objectives to be addressed. This particular skill is critical to keeping projects on time and within budget. The larger the project, the more critical this skill becomes (Grimstad Group, 1995).

One of the most basic aspects of instructional design is the selection of appropriate instructional strategies. This involves selecting appropriate media and delivery systems, and devising activities that promote learner engagement and maintain motivation. However, these decisions can not be made without considering the impact of the instructional context and the nature of the content. It is the one of the most creative parts of the instructional design process.

At this point assessment strategies are also devised and sequenced. All decisions are documented in a design document, and typically the SME and other client representatives are involved in a review process that precedes development activities.

Because instructional design is a highly dynamic and complex and iterative activity, these skills and abilities are often difficult to separate and treat as discrete tasks. They are not completed in a step-by-step fashion in most projects, but are integrated one with the other.

Competency 15. Select or modify existing instructional materials. (Essential) There are five performance statements related to this competency. They are:

   a) *Identify existing instructional materials for reuse or modification consistent with instructional specifications. (Essential)*
   b) *Select materials to support the content analyses, proposed technologies, delivery methods, and instructional strategies. (Essential)*
   c) *Use cost-benefit analyses to decide whether to modify, purchase or develop instructional materials. (Advanced)*
   d) *Work with subject matter experts to validate material selection or modification. (Essential)*
   e) *Integrate existing instructional materials into the design. (Essential)*

All instructional designers should be able to select or modify existing instructional materials. In most situations, there is an emphasis on the modification of materials rather than the creation of new products. It is typically the most cost effective strategy. However, simply taking one set of materials designed for a particular instructional situation and then re-hosting them in a different medium or for a different instructional setting is rarely an effective practice. Competent instructional designers know that there are critical relationships between technologies, delivery methods, learner activities, and content. Every instructional designer must know how to integrate existing instructional materials into an effective instructional design. Often SME's are involved in this process assure the utility of the revised materials in the targeted setting.

While the modification of existing materials is viewed as a basic designer skill, the ability to perform cost-benefit analyses is not. This advanced skill is used to determine whether it is best to modify, purchase or develop entirely new instructional materials in order to accomplish a specific instructional goal. Budget decisions usually are made at higher levels in an organization and are most often associated with positions of responsibility. Those performing critical budget analyses are, therefore, typically the most experienced professionals.

Competency 16. Develop instructional materials. (Essential) This competency has three related performance statements. They are:

a) *Develop materials that support the content analyses, proposed technologies, delivery methods and instructional strategies. (Essential)*

b) *Work with subject matter experts during the development process. (Essential)*

c) *Produce instructional materials in a variety of delivery formats. (Essential)*

Many novice designers have jobs that combine design and development tasks. Consequently, this competency and all three performance statements are categorized as essential. This competency is perhaps the most straightforward of all the 23 competencies, requiring the least elaboration. Nonetheless, the distinctions between design and development should be re-emphasized.

Essentially, design activities involve systematic planning based upon data for instructional products or programs. Development, on the other hand, is the production of those materials. Development may involve writing instructor's and participant guides, or it may involve producing web-based instruction, for example. In large organizations, developers are typically specialists in a particular medium. Although, many designer/developers acquire competence in a variety of delivery formats. These skills are especially useful for those working in small shops.

The development process results in an instructional product that integrates the content, the technology, the delivery methods and the instructional strategies that have been selected and planned in the design phases. Even though development is often a technical activity, it nonetheless may involve interacting with SME's and clients even as is the case in the design and analysis phases of a project. Consequently, all designer/developers must again be able to demonstrate that they can communicate effectively with content specialists.

Competency 17. Design instruction that reflects an understanding of the diversity of learners and groups of learners. (Essential) There are three component performances related to Competency 17. They are:

   a) Design instruction that accommodates different learning styles. (Essential)
   b) Be sensitive to the cultural impact of instructional materials. (Essential)
   c) Accommodate cultural factors that may influence learning in the design. (Essential)

Diversity is a hallmark of many cultures today. Certainly this is true for North America. Such diversity influences the design of instruction even as it impacts other facets of society. Consequently, designers must be sensitive to diversity among learners and to reflect this understanding in their work.

One important way in which learner diversity has been expanding is as the result of globalization. As learning environments become increasingly distributed in nature, there is a corresponding need to understand the many differences among learners and to design instruction accordingly. In some cases, this may involve the design of adaptive learning environments. In nearly all cases it requires the careful analysis of the learner's language, culture, and particular context for learning. This trend is enhanced by the increased use of web-based materials and resources. While some have argued that technology has a dehumanizing effect, the design of instruction that recognizes and respects cultural and linguistic diversity is a particularly humanizing activity.

Another way to integrate learner diversity into an instructional design effort is to design instruction that can accommodate different learning styles (Jonassen and Grabowski 1993). Because much instruction now reaches multi-cultural, multi-linguistic audiences, materials must be designed with sensitivity to cultural issues, and with easily understood language that is not highly idiomatic or laden with jargon.

While some organizations and communities of practice may still involve homogeneous populations of learners, it is increasingly unlikely that this will remain the case. The future appears to hold promise of even more globalization, with access to learning and instruction becoming available any time, any place.

Competency 18. Evaluate and assess instruction and its impact. (Essential) This is a complex competency with nine component performance statements

   a) Construct reliable and valid test items using a variety of formats. (Advanced)

   b) Identify the processes and outcomes to be measured given the identified problem and proposed solutions. (Essential)

   c) Develop and implement formative evaluation plans. (Essential)

   d) Develop and implement summative evaluation plans. (Essential)

   e) Develop and implement confirmative evaluation plans. (Advanced)

   f) Determine the impact of instruction on the organization. (Advanced)

   g) Identify and assess the sources of evaluation data. (Essential)

g) Manage the evaluation process. (Advanced)
i) Discuss and interpret evaluation reports with stakeholders. (Advanced)

Evaluation and assessment has traditionally been considered central to the ID function, and this fact is reflected here. However, while the competency itself is categorized as essential, the associated performance statements are categorized as both essential and advanced. This reflects the view that while assessment and evaluation competence is critical for all designers, particular techniques and processes are difficult and requires expertise and experience.

With respect to evaluation, perhaps the most commonly encountered practices are those associated with formative and summative evaluation. These are standard ID tasks and are usually included in most projects. Even though they are essential tasks, they are often complex. However, all designers should be able to determine the appropriate sources of evaluation data for a particular project.

The most sophisticated evaluation processes center on confirmative evaluation and impact evaluation. Confirmative evaluation seeks to determine if new knowledge and skills have been maintained over time, while impact evaluation determines the impact of a particular instructional intervention on the operation and profits of the target organization. These activities are the purview of experts. Management of the evaluation process, not surprisingly, is also reserved for expert instructional designers, as is reporting and interpreting evaluation findings to customers and others affected by the activity. These skills are all associated with advanced designers with years of experience in positions of responsibility.

The most common assessment task, one expected even of novice designers, is determining exactly which learner performances should be measured in a given situation. Assessment activities characteristics of advanced practitioners, on the other hand, include developing test items and determining that they are both reliable and valid.

Implementation and Management

The competencies in this domain are among those most affected by IBSTPI's decision to expand the model to include advanced competencies as well as core. There are five competency topics addressed in this domain. They are:

- Project management;
- Collaboration;
- Application of business skills;
- Instructional management systems; and
- Implementation of products and programs.

Many of the management competencies are advanced, while the implementation competencies, on the other hand, are mostly essential. This implies that implementation is a competency shared among all designers, even those at the beginning of their career in the field. In this domain, what is being managed varies. In the first three competencies, design and development projects are being managed. In the last two competencies learning is being managed.

This domain frequently includes basic business terms, such as "customer." Every design and development organization has customers, whether they are internal or external to the organization. The "customer" may pay for the design and development with real money, "funny money" (budget transfers within an organization), or no money at all. Here the customer is considered to be the individual or organization that requests the design and development project and has decision-making authority. The customer may also have subject matter expertise and the authority to advise and make decisions on the content of the project.

Competency 19. Plan and manage instructional design projects. (Advanced) This is a complex competency with 10 component performance statements. They are:

a) *Establish project scope and goals. (Advanced)*

b) *Use a variety of techniques and tools to develop a project plan. (Advanced)*

c) *Write project proposals. (Advanced)*

d) *Develop project information systems. (Advanced)*

e) *Monitor multiple instructional design projects. (Advanced)*

f) *Allocate resources to support the project plan. (Advanced)*

g) *Select and manage internal and external consultants. (Advanced)*

h) *Monitor congruence between performance and project plans. (Advanced)*

i) *Troubleshoot project problems. (Advanced)*

j) *Debrief design team to establish lessons learned. (Advanced)*

This competency focuses on the technical aspects of project management. Other competencies in the domain address the people side of project management, and project management as a business skill. At the beginning of a project, planning comes to the fore. Identifying the goal of the project, making sure it is aligned with overall strategy or needs requires more than simply accepting what the customer says. It demands thoughtful reflection and insightful questioning so that one can gain a broad understanding of the environment, culture, and audience. These issues overlap with planning and analysis skills in many respects.

Project planning is complex. While there are estimated ratios of design and development time as compared to instruction for various delivery modes, each organization will have to define its own development ratios based upon their own experiences and particular project requirements. A well-constructed project plan avoids peaks and valleys in the use of resources and provides for adequate but limited reviews and revisions. It should allow for the unexpected, but should not require superhuman efforts to stay on schedule. The plan, along with the budget, assumptions, proposed treatment, and development process are critical parts of a project proposal.

Experienced project managers use a variety of tools, including off-the-shelf project management software, databases to track assets for a multimedia project, or electronic publishing systems that generate various configurations of instructional materials on demand. Moreover, these managers are typically working on multiple projects at one time, or on large single projects that require sub-project coordination. ID managers must be able to deal with interruptions and conflicting demands, even as they make sure customers feel that that they have the manager's undivided attention.

Experienced managers assume that projects will not go according to plan. The manager's challenge is to adjust project milestones, deliverables or other elements of the project, including personnel resources, to achieve the final product. One key resource is the consultant. Whether internal or external, consultants become part of the design team.

Traditional efforts to maintain quality, schedule and budget have been centered on "find-and-fix" approaches. Most ID projects depend on reviews, whether subject matter, design, editorial or others, to "find" problems, then someone, an editor, the developer or designer "fixes" the problem. The project manager's task is to identify and eliminate the causes of project problems.

This knowledge gained from each project experience is extremely valuable to the design and development organization. Capturing, documenting and making that knowledge available helps the organization learn and allows those individuals with less experience to grow from the experience of others.

Competency 20. Promote collaboration, partnerships and relationships among the participants in a design project. (Advanced) The seven components of this competency are:

    a) Identify how and when collaboration and partnerships should be promoted. (Advanced)

    b) Identify stakeholders and the nature of their involvement. (Advanced)

    c) Identify subject matter experts to participate in the design and development process. (Advanced)

    d) Build and promote effective relationships that may impact a design project. (Advanced)

    e) Determine how to use cross functional teams. (Advanced)

    f) Promote and manage the interactions among team members. (Advanced)

    g) Plan for the diffusion of instructional or performance improvement products. (Advanced)

This competency and its associated performance statements reflect an understanding of design projects as inherently cross-functional. These statements stem from the broader notion that successful teams include a broadly representative group of stakeholders and the project is viewed as a collaborative effort. This is not to say that designers yield their professional responsibilities to others. Rather, it says that each stakeholder brings useful understandings and knowledge to the project. Typically, stakeholders are representatives of the customer and other affected groups. Another orientation is to consider any individual or group that could stop a project or limit its success to be a stakeholder.

One way of involving stakeholders is to include them on a project steering committee, even though the actual design and development work is carried out by a team of designers working with subject matter experts and customers. The early and meaningful involvement of customers and other stakeholders increases the probability of successful diffusion, since the affected groups have been part of the decision-making process from the beginning and in a real sense "own" the results.

Competency 21. Apply business skills to managing instructional design. (Advanced). There are eight critical aspects of this competency that need to be demonstrated by the expert designer, typically working in a manager role. They are:

   a) Link design efforts to strategic plans of the organization. (Advanced)

   b) Establish strategic and tactical goals for the design function. (Advanced)

   c) Use a variety of techniques to establish standards of excellence. (Advanced)

   d) Develop a business case to promote the critical role of the design function. (Advanced).

   e) Recruit, retain, and develop instructional design personnel. (Advanced)

   f) Provide financial plans and controls for the instructional design function. (Advanced)

   g) Maintain management and stakeholder support of the design function. (Advanced)

   h) Market services and manage customer relations. (Advanced)

The business skills covered in this competency are planning, managing, budgeting, quality assurance, marketing and advocacy of the design function. Rarely does the design function operate in isolation. Design is always an activity that exists to support the organization's goals. In simplest terms, there should be a corresponding business case for every design activity that in turn is directly linked to the goals of the organization.

The design function should have its own set of goals. They may address issues such as technologies, tools, markets, or services. These goals should be assessed against metrics such as profitability, numbers of people trained or, preferably, measures of improved performance.

Training departments use a variety of processes to demonstrate excellence. These might include the ISO 9000 series of quality standards or specific national standards, like the US government's Baldrige Award criteria. Many use external expert reviews or benchmarking against highly respected organizations. Design or training functions should at least systematically track customer feedback and complaints.

Personnel tasks are also a critical part of the many project manager jobs, although the approaches vary among organizations and between countries. In Australia, Canada, The Netherlands, and the United States for example, recruiting instructional designers is pretty straightforward. There are professional associations and university programs that help with this task. In other countries, such as France and Norway, the role of instructional designer is rare or unheard of. In those countries, the design function may have to rely on developing people into the design role rather than recruiting. In any environment, providing recognition for designers, encouraging growth and development and providing career development opportunities will benefit the design function. Continuous growth and development are crucial to the success of the organization. This is even more true as the instructional design field becomes more dependent on technology.

The financial requirements for the instructional design function are much like those for any project-based entity. There will likely be an overall budget for the design function, along with budgets for each project. Project budgets may or may not be part of the function budget, depending on the policy of the enterprise.

Organizational leaders should see the design and training function as useful and valuable, beyond the business case. This involves building support and creating an understanding of what the design function can do for the enterprise, and then maintaining good relationships with those who engage design services. One aspect of this performance statement relates to positioning, but a substantial part involves understanding customer expectations and meeting or exceeding them consistently.

Competency 22. Design instructional management systems. (Advanced). This competency has four related performance statements – all at the advanced level.

a) *Establish systems for documenting learner progress and course completion. (Advanced)*

b) *Establish systems for maintaining records and issuing reports of individual and group progress. (Advanced)*

c) *Establish systems for diagnosing individual needs and prescribing instructional alternatives. (Advanced)*

There are two types of management systems. Administrative systems handle scheduling, track registrations and completions, and record training hours. Learner-oriented management systems direct the instructional process. They identify the training or instruction needed, monitor learner progress, and record performance data.

A management system must also provide reports to the learner, to the design or training organization, and perhaps to the learner's manager. Group reports may also be generated. In many circumstances designers will not be actually creating the management recording system, but rather they will clarify their requirements and select an existing software product.

Competency 23. Provide for the effective implementation of instructional products and programs. (Essential). There are six components parts of this competency. They are:

a) *Use evaluation data as a guide for revision of products and programs. (Advanced)*

b) *Update instructional products and programs as required. (Essential)*

c) *Monitor and revise the instructional delivery process as required. (Essential)*

d) *Revise instructional products and programs to reflect changes in professional practice or policy. (Essential)*

e) Revise instructional products and programs to reflect changes in the organization or the target population. (Essential)

f) Recommend plans for organizational support of instructional programs. (Advanced)

Instructional design is a process directed not simply towards product development, but toward product use as well. Consequently, it is important to monitor the ongoing operation of instructional interventions and to revise materials and programs as necessary. Revisions may be required in the content, sequencing, case examples, and possibly in the delivery systems.

Some problems demand immediate changes, such as a "bug" in a multimedia program that prevents learners from proceeding. Other problems can wait for scheduled, systematic revisions, while still others may require no action at all.

This competency is the only skill area in the Implementation and Management domain that is essential for all designers, even those with little or no experience. Designers must be sensitive to changing needs of learners and organizations, to accuracy and timeliness of content, and to the implications of changing delivery resources.

However, there are implementation tasks that require the sophistication, political sensitivity and astuteness of senior designers. The interpretation and use of evaluation data is one such area. Another pertains to strategies for obtaining or maintaining organizational support for the intervention. Leadership changes and new internal or external pressures in the workplace can radically alter the effectiveness of a previously successful program. More comprehensive and strategic remedies may be necessary for these situations. Advanced design expertise is required.

Conclusions

Presently instructional design is a complex, problem-solving process that requires technical skill, "people" skills, and political savvy. Instructional design is not the simple, almost intuitive task assumed by some outside of the field. In addition, good design often requires a substantial amount of experience in a given industry or organization.

The newly revised ID competencies describe these skills in a very concrete manner. Their value, however, goes beyond merely describing and defining the field. When put to work, these competencies can advance the profession and facilitate organizational growth. Chapter 4 examines ways in which this can be accomplished.

The Use of ID Competencies

With Robert C. Roberts

There are at least four categories of professionals who can use these competencies in their work. These are:

- Design practitioners;
- Design managers;
- Design-oriented academics; and
- Professional development suppliers.

Each is likely to approach the competencies with differing needs, and consequently use them in a unique manner. The practitioners may use them for benchmarking, the managers for human resource functions and leading projects, the academics and consultants for curriculum development.

The ID competencies do more than describe designers' skills and knowledge. They describe job requirements and provide a common language for the field that transcends cultural boundaries. In a sense, they define the field of instructional design. Competency models provide guidance for those entering the field, as well as for veterans seeking professional updating and improvement. They can even suggest the parameters of specialty areas and direction for improvement of the designer's organization.

This chapter will examine the major uses of the ID competencies by these four groups of professionals. In addition, it will explore the issues surrounding the certification of instructional designers. This is a phenomenon that has long been debated within the ID community and is once again surfacing in today's marketplace. Whether one favors the practice or not, certification is inevitably linked to competency identification.

ID Competency Utility

Competency Use by Practicing Designers

Planning for Individual Professional Development. Consumers of instructional design services are becoming increasingly sophisticated and have higher performance expectations for designers. Consequently, those in the design field are forced to upgrade their skills to remain competitive. These 2000 ID competencies can provide direction in this process, thereby advancing individual careers and adding value to organizations. In essence, the competencies and performance statements can serve as robust criteria for professional development planning. This is possible given their established content validity and the fact that they highlight exactly how the profession is evolving and define those skills now expected in the marketplace. The competencies provide a reference point for the coming decade and as such provide a framework for professional development efforts. They provide designers a means of comparing their own competence and performance capabilities against an external benchmark established by professional peer groups.

One can use the questions in Table 4.1 as a guide for professional development planning. These questions can be used to structure self-assessments of one's needs and help plan for ways of filling skill and knowledge gaps. Such self-assessments can be conducted in addition to routine performance assessments, or when one is preparing for advanced graduate study or selecting professional development workshops.

Novice and experienced designers may use this self-assessment in different ways. Novices might focus on the particular competencies required for a specific upcoming project or when preparing for a particular position to which they aspire or for enhancing one's employability when changing jobs.

Experienced designers, especially those designers who received their formal training some time ago, typically have other concerns. This self-assessment process may be particularly important when they need to update their skill sets. They may be deficient in performance analysis techniques, or technology skills, for example. The competencies and performance statements may

Table 4.1 Questions for Analyzing ID Professional Development Needs

Question	Yes	No
1 Do I require this competency or capability to perform my current job assignments?		
2 Do I require this competency or performance capability for future work assignments or promotional opportunities?		
3 Is this competency or performance statement one for which I have a particular talent or interest?		
4 Do I have this competency or performance capability?		
5 Can I perform at the appropriate level of proficiency?		
6 If needed, can I acquire the competency or capability in a professional development program?		

introduce new terms and concepts currently used in the field. These experienced designers may wish to focus upon those competencies that allow one to facilitate specialization in one aspect of the design process. Acquisition of these competencies can facilitate the transition from a generalist design role to that of a specialist. These are some specific ways in which the competencies can be used as a basis for in-depth professional development and acquiring advanced levels of design expertise.

Competency Use by Design Managers

Instructional design managers are another group acutely concerned with designer competence. It is important not only to personnel and project management, but is often critical to building a department and aligning it within the organization at large.

Managing Human Resource Functions. The competencies can be useful for managers as they engage in a variety of human resource activities. First, they can serve as guidelines for the formation or revision of job descriptions and career development models. Used in this fashion, the competencies can help designers and project managers alike. Designers can see what skills are required in a particular position and then determine if they are likely to be promoted through the various levels once on the job. Managers can similarly use them as aids in the recruitment and hiring of new designers to help insure that prospective employees have those skills and knowledge required of a given position. The 2000 competencies are particularly useful for these purposes since they distinguish between those skills needed by novice and experienced professionals. Moreover, they can highlight those specific skills needed for more focused design roles, such as an analyst or project manager.

Similarly, the competencies can also be used as a basis for selecting external consultants or vendors. This is increasingly important with the heavy reliance upon outsourcing and the corresponding proliferation of freelance instructional designers. The process for using the competencies for vendor selection parallels their use with permanent employees.

Managers can also use the competencies to offer specific job performance feedback to practicing designers. The competencies can form the basis of performance appraisals, mentoring and coaching programs. The competencies offer a framework for planning the further development of individuals, as well as intact design teams. This form of assessment provides the manager with insight into department strengths and weaknesses. It may lead to identifying needs for further professional development, or perhaps for hiring additional staff or outsourcing of particular design roles. This identification is particularly important when an organization begins to transition from a training development mindset to a performance improvement consulting approach. Such radical transformations in process and mindset demand systematic examination of the organization's composite skill sets, and planning for complete upgrading in those newly required skills and knowledge.

Managing Projects and Teams. Today much of the work in a complex training operation is team-based. These teams are typically cross-functional and it is important for the designer capabilities to be fully covered in the team. In addition, it is increasingly the case that these teams are virtual, which puts a premium on communication and technology skills. The ID competencies can guide project managers when they form these project teams. They can be used to more precisely select designers who possess specific required skill sets. Team members can be selected by referring to the competencies to insure the team has the range of knowledge and skills needed for the project. Using the competencies in this manner will allow an organization to "custom build" project teams capable of performing successful assignments. They can also serve as guidelines for directing the team, and pointing to the need for additional team resources.

Benchmarking. Benchmarking is now a standard activity in small and large organizations. The new ID competencies can play a role in this process as well. Managers wishing to benchmark their design group against leaders in the field can use the competencies as the standard of excellence by which they can compare themselves to similar organizations. When used this way the competencies allow an organization to verify their level of excellence by providing evidence that they comply with the standards set by the IBSTPI ID competencies and performance statements.

Educating Management. In many organizations, leaders and managers are not familiar with instructional systems design, or the degree of knowledge, skill and experience needed to design and implement effective instructional design projects. An important part of a manager's role then is to educate upper management and the competencies can be used as an external authority in this process. Often such explanations are imperative if a department is to receive the resources they need to be successful. For example, a design team may be capable of designing instruction that produces the intended learning outcomes, but display little capability to conduct an impact evaluation that assesses the effect of a particular intervention on the organization. The

Table 4.2 Questions for Persons Managing ID Functions

Question	Yes	No
1 Do the job descriptions of members of the current ID department or team reflect the range of competencies required?		
2 Do current employees demonstrate the design competence required for their particular jobs?		
3 Do the team members have the competencies required for an upcoming project?		
4 Does the prospective employee have the specific skills required for the position?		
5 Do the competencies of the prospective employee complement those of the department or team?		
6 Has the prospective consultant or vendor provided evidence of competence in the specific needed areas?		
7 Is it clear to others within and outside of the organization the range of competence and capabilities of the department or team?		

manager in this scenario can use the competencies as an external standard to define the complexities of the task to higher-level management and thus demonstrate the need for additional resources for the design team.

Managers may use the questions in Table 4.2 as a guide for addressing the various personnel and project management issues that can be influenced by these competencies.

Competency Use by Academics

The competencies can also be useful tools for those who prepare future instructional designers. Typically these persons are college and university faculty. The ID competencies then can serve as guides for curriculum development, program revision, and accreditation.

Developing and Updating ID Curricula. The most comprehensive preparation of instructional designers takes place in graduate university programs, usually in an Instructional or Educational Technology programs, or perhaps in a Human Resource Development program. These programs are shaped, to a great extent, by the skills needed in the marketplace, the literature of the field, and the capabilities and vision of the faculty. The new IBSTPI ID competencies are useful tools for pinpointing the skills currently demanded in the workplace. The competencies serve as a means of articulation between universities and the consumers of ID services.

The competencies can serve as program goals, while the performance statements can provide the basis for course objectives. In addition, the domains may lend themselves to course construction. For example, Professional Foundation competencies are especially pertinent to introductory courses and the Implementation and Management competencies are pertinent to advanced courses such as project management.

Once the structure of a designer preparation curriculum is in place, the competencies can provide input to faculty teaching the various classes. This is especially true with respect to the assessment of student progress. The performance statements can provide particular direction to not only traditional forms of assessment, but also to students who are developing portfolios that demonstrate their new capabilities. It is possible for the competencies to suggest learning activities related to the various skills within each of the major design domains.

The competencies can also be used as a basis for the review and revision of existing curricula, typically an ongoing task. The competencies can be used to assess a program's currency, completeness and depth. Faculty members may wish to use the questions in Table 4.3 as they review their curriculum by comparing it to the IBSTPI ID competencies.

Accrediting ID Programs. Most academic programs must conduct periodic self-studies and be reviewed by internal and external accrediting bodies. While such bodies typically have general guidelines and standards to which the department must respond, it is often possible for programs to identify more

Table 4.3 Questions for University Faculty Reviewing Curriculum

Question	Yes	No
1 Does the curriculum address each of the essential competency skill areas?		
2 Do the advanced courses address the competencies required by experienced designers?		
3 Are the competencies used to advise students who are interested in preparing for more specialized designer positions?		
4 Are the competencies used as a guide to place students in internships and work-study programs?		
5 Does the curriculum address the professional development needs of graduates currently working as design practitioners?		
6 Are additional faculty needed to adequately address the range of competencies required in the current market?		

specific criteria that more directly address their missions. These standards, however, must be authoritative and valid for each field. Departments can easily use the IBSTPI ID competencies as they analyze and document their programs. In this way, they can use the competencies as a basis for benchmarking best design practice and demonstrate that they provide instruction that is directed toward the development of proficiency in the most critical aspects of the instructional design field.

Forming Research Agendas. A primary part of academic work focuses on research. While research agendas are largely dependent upon individual interests and expertise, the ID competencies can provide some direction to research plans. These competencies identify the scope and emphases of current design practice. As such, they provide a comprehensive list of topics and skills important to practicing professionals. Research addressing any of these topics is more likely to be attuned to the concerns and needs of the practitioner community.

However, there are specific research questions suggested by these competencies. Some of these are:

- How do societal, business and technological changes impact the evolution of these ID competencies?
- To what extent can the processes embedded in these competencies be validated in natural work settings?
- What is the impact of evolving views of human learning on the ID competencies?
- What is the relationship, if any, between organization size and culture on the competency profiles of designers?
- To what extent do persons in related fields (such as organizational development) demonstrate instructional design competence?

Competency Use by Professional Development Suppliers

While most in the field would prefer that all instructional designers hold advanced degrees and have received formal intensive instructional design education and training, there are large numbers of practitioners who do not have this background. It is not unusual for designers to have extensive subject matter or industry-specific expertise, and have been recruited internally into the training department. Design "expertise" then comes from on-the-job experience, modeling others, and often attending short workshops on ID techniques and processes offered by private providers. Those who develop and offer such workshops will find these competencies particularly useful.

Consultants providing professional development training for practicing instructional designers may use the competencies and performance statements in much the same manner as university faculty, but with a somewhat different focus. For example, professional development workshops and seminars can be built around specific skill areas, such as needs assessment, evaluation and the legal and ethical competencies required by experienced designers.

It is especially critical to the commercial success of design consultants that their professional development offerings are authoritative and of the highest

Table 4.4 Questions for Consultants Planning ID Professional Development

Issues		Yes	No
1	Does the workshop address those areas of design most applicable to this group of designers or for most designers without formal graduate training?		
2	Does the workshop address those areas of design in which most practitioners need updating?		
3	Does the workshop address the specific needs of specialized designers?		
4	Is there a sequence among the workshops offered that matches the growth of novice designers into expert designers?		
5	Are the workshop objectives, instructional strategies and practice opportunities logically supported by the competencies and performance statements in a given domain?		
6	Are learners assessed on skills most essential to design success?		

quality. This external validation can be provided by basing such instruction on the IBSTPI ID competencies. Specifically, the competencies can be linked to a series of offerings by using the questions in Table 4.4 to plan professional development training for designers with little formal education or training in the field.

The competencies can also serve as the basis for the review of these professional development programs.

When commercial training programs are built and updated around a pre-specified set of public competencies, not only do the courses acquire valued authenticity, but prospective trainees can use these same competencies as a gauge for selecting the workshops. With the competencies, trainees (and their employers) are able to more precisely match the training with their particular skill needs.

ID Competencies and Designer Certification

A topic of recurring interest to designer practitioners and design managers alike is that of professional certification. This is not an issue without controversy. Nonetheless, it is one that has again aroused new interest. Professional certification has been defined as a voluntary process by which a professional association or organization measures and reports on the degree of competence of individual practitioners (Gilley, Geis and Seyfer, 1987).

The Case for Certification

The intent of certification is to inform the public that individuals who have achieved certification have demonstrated a particular degree of knowledge and skill. It offers title protection, as only those who are certified may use a particular title. It is one method of protecting the public (Browning, Bugbee and Mullins, 1996). Functionally, professional certification constitutes a formal and public definition of a profession. One outcome of professional certification is the ability to distinguish between those who have demonstrated competency, in an agreed upon manner, and those who have not. Another is the promotion of ongoing professional competency.

Professional certification can enhance the reputation and public image of the profession, even as it seeks to protect the public and employers from incompetent practitioners. This is one key reason certification is supported by many. This is, typically, accomplished by requiring persons to be judged competent by their peers at a predetermined criterion before they can practice the profession. In most cases, the basis upon which the judgment is made is a professional certification exam. Since there are continual changes in knowledge and performance expectations, the criterion for demonstrating competency is typically revised from time to time. This evolving criteria maintains the most current definition of competence for the profession.

The development of a criterion for professional certification can promote three immediate and desirable outcomes. First, it establishes a basis for selecting new members of the profession. Second, it establishes a sound basis for training new members, and third it can establish a basis for upgrading the skills of current practitioners. Overall, these outcomes can result in a general improvement in the competence of those individuals who practice instructional design.

These perceptions of quality are likely to increase the confidence of consumers of instructional design services in the profession. Correspondingly, employers will have a clear basis for selecting and managing the work of instructional designers. Peer certification can increase the confidence of many external groups in a given profession. Members of the medical, legal, engineering and business communities have created professional certification procedures for their fields and have achieved many of these desirable goals. There are many who would like instructional designers to follow suit.

Certification Issues

When considering the prospect of professional certification for instructional designers, several issues need to be explored. First, who is being certified? It is clear from the nature of the 2000 IBSTPI competencies that there is no longer just one concept of an instructional designer. There are novice designers, and there are experienced designers. Moreover, there are specialists in various aspects of instructional design. Each group has different skills.

Does this imply that separate certification procedures are then necessary for these assorted groups? Do novices require different testing instruments than experienced designers. Or is there only a need for an "entry level" professional certification based upon the essential competencies? Should certification be available that is skewed to the skills of specialists in the field? The answers are not readily apparent to the profession.

While many welcome certification as a way of upgrading the field, others feel threatened by the prospect. They may feel their livelihood is at risk if they do not choose to take on the time and expense of certification. Other successful practitioners may not satisfy the certification requirements when they are embedded in formal testing situations. For these reasons, it is not unusual for some professional groups to recommend that current practitioners be "grandfathered" into the system and not be required to meet certification standards. Such procedures, however, can lead to a situation in which public assurances of competency apply to only parts of the professional group, typically the newer members. This, in turn, makes the issues of civil and legal liability of organizations even more difficult to manage.

There have also been some academics who have questioned the value of designer certification. Their reasoning has been three-fold in nature. First, they feel that the conferring of a graduate degree in the field does provide a type of certification, and that other "add-on's" are superfluous. However, many have more technical reservations. They have expressed concerns over difficulties with the testing and measurement upon which the certification would be based. These latter issues are real. Testing abstracted from demonstrated actual skills is of only minimal value, and portfolios of work are difficult to assemble given the nature of much practice. Organizations have proprietary rights to the products and much of the work in completed not by individuals, but by design teams. Third, some reservations with designer certification stem from a conviction that the instructional design process is simply too complex a task to lend itself to uniform testing and certification.

Finally, no certification process can be instituted without costs, either to the organization or to the individual. These monies are typically paid to a professional organization that manages the certification procedures and maintains records of who is certified, who has been re-certified and, who has been decertified. These administrative costs are usually borne by the individuals who are certified. They can be substantial investments, and some question whether they are merited in light of the future earnings that might be generated by the new credential. Some see the costs as being beneficial for those without formal university training in instructional design, but less valuable for those who have earned a graduate degree in the field. All of these issues have yet to be resolved.

Conclusions

A variety of uses for the ID competencies have been suggested in this chapter. They can be used by design practitioners, design managers, design-oriented academics and professional development consultants. This is not an exhaustive list, however. Prospective students, for example, can use these competencies as a basis for evaluating the utility of a given academic program. There are likely other applications of these competencies as well.

There is an underlying assumption that their use should transcend geographical setting, organization, and to some extent time. This is not only because of the generic character of the competencies and performance statements, but also because of the ability for particular users to customize them without a concomitant loss of integrity. Still the competencies provide a common design language as well as a common set of skills. This allows them to be "transported" to many settings.

Even though the competencies as a whole are comprehensive, they can also be viewed from the perspective of those in the various design specialty fields. This orientation will be discussed in Chapter 5.

The Competencies and ID Specialization

A competent and experienced instructional designer can demonstrate the skills associated with the systematic design process and is therefore capable of managing a design project from needs assessment through the design, development, implementation and evaluation phases. In many organizations instructional designers continue to perform all five phases of a design project, but there is an increasing trend towards specialization, especially in large organizations. This is the result of a number of factors. The profession itself is becoming more complex and sophisticated, which in turn leads to specialization. As an example, the shift from designing for a classroom instructor to designing technology-based instruction has led to the emergence of multi-media designers and this is rapidly evolving into the E-learning specialist. Similarly, the transition from a training focus to a performance improvement consulting approach highlights the necessity for strong performance analysis skills, and in many large organizations this has led to a specialization in analysis. Management's emphasis on accountability and evidence of return on the investment has also resulted in a greater emphasis on evaluation and measurement.

Increased use of ID specialists can also be attributed to the globalization of companies to a great extent since globalization has led to a huge increase in the size of the population to be trained. In some organizations it is not unusual for tens of thousands of people located in more than a dozen countries to require the same training. In such cases a single designer cannot handle a project of this size and a design team is established. The teams typically include content experts from technical groups in the organization, as well as specialists from other fields such as Human Resources, Organizational Development, Information Technology, Marketing, and Communications. While many teams continue to use generalist designers, there is often a group of instructional designers on the team who specialize in certain aspects of the ID process.

At the same time, there is a trend in many large organizations to downsize and build a leaner work force. As a consequence, much of the instructional design work is now being outsourced. This leads to the use of an internal designer specializing in project management. Often this person is managing several projects simultaneously.

The Nature of ID Specialization

There are a number of established or emerging specialist roles in the field of instructional design. Four roles – analyst, evaluator, E-learning specialist, and project manager – have evolved and are common in many settings. They are:

- *The Analyst* – specializing in performance analysis and training needs assessment;
- *The Evaluator* – specializing in various forms of evaluation and assessment, but especially transfer and impact evaluation;
- *The E-learning Specialist* – specializing in development of multimedia and electronic learning products, particularly web-based learning; and
- *The Project Manager* – specializing in managing internal and/or external designers on one or several projects.

Although these are not the only specialist roles in the field, they are the most widely recognizable ones. In some organizations, these roles may be combined or separated depending upon project and organizational idiosyncrasies. For example, the the E-learning specialist role as described here may be apportioned into several specialist roles for large projects, or the E-learning specialist may double as the project manager. It is far more likely that these ID specialists will be found in large, rather than small, organizations.

These specializations do not downgrade or supplant the role of the generalist instructional designer. Generalist designers are still the norm in small organizations, and even in larger work settings the generalist has a necessary role. For example, general strategy selection decisions are typically generalist tasks, and generalists construct design documents. Specialists do not assume all design tasks.

The competencies that are required by each of the major specialist roles are identified in Table 5.1. The designations in Table 5.1 were made and then validated by generalist and specialist designers from business, government and academe in the United States and the United Kingdom.

Some of the competencies are termed "primary" (designated by an upper case "P") and some are labeled as "supporting" (designated by a lower case "s"). Primary competencies are those that are most critical to the specialization. A specialist designer requires special skills in the primary competency areas. The supporting ones, while necessary, are usually not as central to the performance of the role in most job situations. The mature specialist will be able to demonstrate both the primary and supporting competencies. In addition, design specialists typically have an in-depth knowledge all of the essential design skills, as well as an understanding of the other specializations. They are aware of the relationships among the various roles, and have an appreciation for cross-specialization.

In Table 5.1 the extensive overlap in competencies of the analyst and the evaluator is obvious, and these commonalties make it advantageous for these roles to be assumed by the same person in some work situations. Consequently, three ID specialist roles will be examined in this chapter:

- The Analyst/Evaluator;
- The E-learning specialist; and
- The Project Manager.

Within each of these three roles, the various required skills have been grouped into the four competency domains – Professional Foundations, Planning and Analysis, Design and Development, and Implementation and Management.

Table 5.1 ID Specialist Roles: Primary and Supporting Competencies

	ANALYST	EVALUATOR	E-LEARNING SPECIALIST	PROJECT MANAGER
PROFESSIONAL FOUNDATIONS				
1 Communicate effectively in visual, oral and written form.	P	P	P	P
a. Create messages that accommodate learner needs and characteristics, content, and objectives.			P	
b. Write and edit text to produce messages that are clear, concise, and grammatically correct.	P	P	P	
c. Apply principles of message design to page layout and screen design.			P	
d. Create or select visuals that instruct, orient, or motivate.			P	
e. Deliver presentations that effectively engage and communicate.	P	P	P	
f. Use active listening skills in all situations.	P	P	S	S
g. Present and receive information in a manner that is appropriate for the norms and tasks of the group or team.	P	P	P	P
h. Seek and share information and ideas among individuals with diverse backgrounds and roles.	P	P		
i. Facilitate meetings effectively.	P	P	S	P
2 Apply current research and theory to the practice of instructional design.		S	S	
a. Promote, apply and disseminate the results of instructional design theory and research.				
b. Read instructional design research, theory and practice literature.		S	S	
c. Apply concepts, techniques and theory of other disciplines to problems of learning, instruction and instructional design.			S	
3 Update and improve one's skills, knowledge and attitudes pertaining to instructional design and related fields.	S		S	
a. Apply developments in instructional design and related fields.	S		S	
b. Acquire and apply new technology skills to instructional design practice.			P	
c. Participate in professional activities.				
d. Document one's work as a foundation for future efforts, publications or professional presentation.			S	S
e. Establish and maintain contacts with other professionals.				
4 Apply fundamental research skills to instructional design projects.	P	P		
a. Use a variety of data collection tools and procedures.	P	P		
b. Apply appropriate research methodologies to needs assessment and evaluation.	P	P		

continued

Table 5.1   ID Specialist Roles: Primary and Supporting Competencies   continued

		ANALYST	EVALUATOR	E-LEARNING SPECIALIST	PROJECT MANAGER
c.	Use basic statistical techniques in needs assessment and evaluation.	P	P		
d.	Write research and evaluation reports.	P	P		
5	Identify and resolve ethical and legal implications of design in the workplace.			s	s
a.	Identify ethical and legal dimensions of instructional design practice.				s
b.	Anticipate and respond to ethical consequences of design decisions.				s
c.	Recognize and respect intellectual property rights of others.			P	s
d.	Recognize the ethical and legal implications and consequences of instructional products.			s	s
e.	Adhere to regulatory guidelines and organizational policies.				s
6	Conduct a needs assessment.	P			
a.	Describe the problem and its dimensions, identifying the discrepancies between current and desired performance.	P			
b.	Clarify the varying perceptions of need and their implications.	P			
c.	Select and use appropriate needs assessment tools and techniques.	P			
d.	Determine the possible causes of the problem and potential solutions.	P			
e.	Recommend and advocate non-instructional solutions when appropriate.	P			
f.	Complete a cost benefit analysis for recommended solutions.	s			
7	Design a curriculum or program.				
a.	Determine the scope of the curriculum or program.				s
b.	Specify courses based upon needs assessment outcomes.				
c.	Sequence courses for learners and groups of learners.				
d.	Analyze and modify existing curricula or programs to insure adequate content coverage.				
e.	Modify an existing curriculum to reflect changes in society, the knowledge base, technology, and or the organization.				
8	Select and use a variety of techniques for determining instructional content.				
a.	Identify content requirements in accordance with needs assessment findings.				
b.	Elicit, synthesize and validate content from subject matter experts and other sources.				

Table 5.1   ID Specialist Roles: Primary and Supporting Competencies   continued

		ANALYST	EVALUATOR	E-LEARNING SPECIALIST	PROJECT MANAGER
c.	Determine the breadth and depth of intended content coverage given instructional constraints.				
d.	Determine prerequisites given the type of subject matter, the needs of the learners and the organization.				
e.	Use appropriate techniques to analyze varying types of content.				
9	Identify and describe target population characteristics.	P		P	
a.	Determine characteristics of the target population influencing learning and transfer.	P		P	
b.	Analyze, evaluate and select learner profile data relevant to a particular design situation.	P		s	
10	Analyze the characteristics of the environment.	P	P	s	
a.	Identify aspects of the physical and social environments that impact the delivery of instruction.	P	P	P	
b.	Identify environmental and cultural aspects that influence attitudes toward instructional interventions.	P	P	P	
c.	Identify environmental and cultural factors that influence learning, attitudes, and performance.	P	P	s	
d.	Identify the nature and role of varying work environments in the teaching and learning process.	P	P		
e.	Determine the extent to which organizational mission, philosophy and values influence the design, implementation and success of a project.	P	P		s
11	Analyze the characteristics of existing and emerging technologies and their use in an instructional environment.			P	
a.	Specify the capabilities of existing and emerging technologies to enhance motivation, visualization, interaction, simulation, and individualization.			P	
b.	Evaluate the capacity of a given infrastructure to support selected technologies.			P	S
c.	Assess the benefits of existing and emerging technologies.			P	
12	Reflect upon the elements of a situation before finalizing design solutions and strategies.	s	s	s	s
a.	Generate multiple solutions to a given problem situation.	P			
b.	Remain open to alternative solutions until sufficient data have been collected and verified.				s
c.	Assess the consequences and implications of design decisions on the basis of prior experience, intuition and knowledge.			s	
d.	Revisit selected solutions continuously and adjust as necessary.			s	

continued

Table 5.1   ID Specialist Roles: Primary and Supporting Competencies   continued

	ANALYST	EVALUATOR	E-LEARNING SPECIALIST	PROJECT MANAGER
DESIGN AND DEVELOPMENT				
13 Select, modify, or create a design and development model appropriate for a given project.				
a. Consider multiple design and development models.				
b. Select or create a model suitable for the project based on an analysis of model elements.				
c. Modify the model if project parameters change.				
d. Provide a rationale for the selected design and development model.				
14 Select and use a variety of techniques to define and sequence the instructional content and strategies.			S	
a. Use appropriate techniques to identify the conditions that determine the scope of the instructional content.				
b. Use appropriate techniques to specify and sequence instructional goals and objectives.				
c. Select appropriate media and delivery systems.			P	
d. Analyze the learning outcomes and select appropriate strategies.			s	
e. Analyze the instructional context and select appropriate strategies.			s	
f. Select appropriate participation and motivational strategies.			s	
g. Select and sequence assessment techniques.		P	s	
h. Prepare a design document and circulate for review and approval.			s	
15 Select or modify existing instructional materials.			P	
a. Identify existing instructional materials for reuse or modification consistent with instructional specifications.			P	
b. Select materials to support the content analyses, proposed technologies, delivery methods and instructional strategies.			P	
c. Use cost-benefit analyses to decide whether to modify, purchase or developing instructional materials.			P	
d. Work with subject matter experts to validate material selection or modification.				
e. Integrate existing instructional materials into the design.				
16 Develop instructional materials.			P	
a. Develop materials that support the content analyses, proposed technologies, delivery methods, and instructional strategies.			P	

Table 5.1 ID Specialist Roles: Primary and Supporting Competencies   continued

		ANALYST	EVALUATOR	E-LEARNING SPECIALIST	PROJECT MANAGER
b.	Work with subject matter experts during the development process.			P	
c.	Produce instructional materials in a variety of delivery formats.				
17	Design instruction that reflects an understanding of the diversity of learners and groups of learners.			P	
a.	Design instruction that accommodates different learning styles.			P	
b.	Be sensitive to the cultural impact of instructional materials.			P	
c.	Accommodate cultural factors that may influence learning in the design.			P	
18	Evaluate and assess instruction and its impact.		P		
a.	Construct reliable and valid test items using a variety of formats.		P		
b.	Identify the processes and outcomes to be measured given the identified problem and proposed solutions.		P		
c.	Develop and implement formative evaluation plans.		P		
d.	Develop and implement summative evaluation plans.		P		
e.	Develop and implement confirmative evaluation plans.		P		
f.	Determine the impact of instruction on the organization.		P		
g.	Identify and assess the sources of evaluation data.		P		
h.	Manage the evaluation process.		P		
i.	Discuss and interpret evaluation reports with stakeholders.		P		
IMPLEMENTATION AND MANAGEMENT					
19	Plan and manage instructional design projects.				P
a.	Establish project scope and goals.				P
b.	Use a variety of techniques to develop a project plan.				P
c.	Write project proposals.				P
d.	Develop project information systems				P
e.	Monitor multiple instructional design projects				P
f.	Allocate resources to support the project plan.				P
g.	Select and manage internal and external consultants.				P
h.	Monitor congruence between performance and project plans.				P
i.	Troubleshoot project problems.				P

continued

Table 5.1   ID Specialist Roles: Primary and Supporting Competencies   continued

		ANALYST	EVALUATOR	E-LEARNING SPECIALIST	PROJECT MANAGER
j.	Debrief design team to establish lessons learned.		s		P
20	Promote collaboration, partnerships and relationships among the participants in a design project.	s			P
a.	Identify how and when collaboration and partnerships should be promoted.	s			P
b.	Identify stakeholders and the nature of their involvement.	P			P
c.	Identify subject matter experts to participate in the design and development process.	s			s
d.	Build and promote effective relationships that may impact a design project.	s		s	P
e.	Determine how to use cross-functional teams.				s
f.	Promote and manage the interactions among team members.				P
g.	Plan for the diffusion of instructional or performance improvement products.				P
21	Apply business skills to managing instructional design.				s
a.	Link design efforts to the strategic plans of the organization.	P	P	P	P
b.	Establish strategic and tactical goals for the design function.				
c.	Use a variety of techniques to establish standards of excellence.				
d.	Develop a business case to promote the critical role of the design function.				
e.	Recruit, retain, and develop instructional design personnel.				
f.	Provide financial plans and controls for the instructional design function.				s
g.	Maintain management and stakeholder support of the design function.				s
h.	Market services and manage customer relations.				s
22	Design instructional management systems.			s	
a.	Establish systems for documenting learner progress and course completion.				
b.	Establish systems for maintaining records and issuing reports of individual and group progress.				
c.	Establish systems for diagnosing individual needs and prescribing instructional alternatives.				
23	Provide for the effective implementation of instructional products and programs.			s	s
a.	Use evaluation data as a guide for revision of products and programs.			P	s

Table 5.1   ID Specialist Roles: Primary and Supporting Competencies   continued

	ANALYST	EVALUATOR	E-LEARNING SPECIALIST	PROJECT MANAGER
b. Update instructional products and programs as required.			s	
c. Monitor and revise the instructional delivery process as required.			s	
d. Revise instructional products and programs to reflect changes in professional practice or policy.			s	
e. Revise instructional products and programs to reflect changes in the organization or target population.			s	
f. Recommend plans for organizational support of instructional programs.				s

The Analyst/Evaluator

Analyst/evaluators play dual roles in a project. As analysts, they specialize in performance analysis and training needs assessment. These activities occur at the 'front end' of the instructional design process. As evaluators, they work in all project phases – conducting formative evaluations during design and development and conducting summative and confirmation evaluations during implementation. Aspects of each of the four ID competency domains are pertinent to the analyst/evaluator. The analyst/evaluator competencies relate to:

- Professional Foundations, with particular emphasis on communication and research skills;
- Planning and Analysis, with particular emphasis on identifying learner and environmental characteristics and conducting needs assessment;
- Design and Development, with particular emphasis on evaluation methods; and
- Implementation and Management, with particular emphasis on working with project stakeholders and linking recommendations to the strategic goals of the organization.

Professional Foundation Skills

Analyst/evaluators, like all instructional designers, are dependent upon a broad range of foundational skills. Remaining current in terms of both new tools and techniques and emerging theory is critical to every aspect of this rather technical area of specialization. However, the most important areas of competence pertain to communication and research.

Communication. A high level of competency in communication skills is critical to the analyst/evaluator because the data collected through interviews, focus groups and surveys become the foundation for all major design, development and revision decisions.   In most cases (see Table 5.1) the primary communication competencies for the analyst are the same as those of the evaluator, but they are expressed in different ways to achieve different ends.

Communication competencies specific to analyst/evaluation specialists are all primary competencies. They center on the need to interact with individuals and diverse groups throughout the organization when gathering data and insight into "what is really going on".   Active listening is an especially important competency.   Analyst/evaluators interact with individuals and groups as they gather information, and the ability to listen and actually "hear" what informants are telling them is critical.

In the data collection phase of an ID project, analysts must lay aside their preconceived ideas about the issues at hand. Instead, they rely on active listening and expert facilitation skills to uncover data about optimal and actual performance and root causes of the problem. They may discuss issues pertaining to motivation and openness to change, the target group's attitudes to potential solutions including delivery systems, and work environment factors that may affect the choice of intervention.

At the conclusion of the data collection phase analyst/evaluators prepare a report and in many cases will also make a presentation of the findings to stakeholder groups. They must prepare crisp, well-written, well-documented reports using graphical displays of data to advantage. Reports should be written in the customer's language rather than instructional design terminology, in order to gain the attention of management decision-makers as well as customers. For example, in engineering organizations needs assessment is better referred to as requirements gathering; in some organizations the term evaluation has been replaced by results assessment.

Analyst/evaluation specialists require a high level of expertise in making a well-reasoned and compelling case for change. Presentations to senior management and other stakeholders must be informative, engaging and persuasive, convincing them the proposed solutions are compatible with and responsive to the needs and goals of the organization. Recommendations should be data-based, but the analyst/evaluator also needs the "people" skills to gain support for them.

The design team is one of the analyst/evaluator's primary customers. Team members use the findings and recommendations to make significant design and development decisions. The team requires clearly communicated information about the learner group characteristics, environmental or cultural factors they may need to accommodate in the design and development process, and the anticipated degree of support for specific interventions. When undertaking revisions the design team relies on evaluation data and recommendations.

Likewise, the design team is likely to depend on the analyst/evaluator for debriefing them to establish project lessons learned. Since evaluations are usually undertaken some time after the instructional event, face-to-face meetings between the design team and the analyst/evaluator are generally necessary to meaningfully discuss the report and gain insights from the evaluation. Such meetings can be used to enhance future course development as well as suggest revisions in the current program.

Research. Although analysis and evaluation are typically not considered research, these tasks have many similarities to the research endeavor. The core of the analyst/evaluator's work is data collection and analysis, and there is a critical array of research competencies required for these jobs. Whereas the evaluator seeks to uncover issues after the intervention, the analyst seeks to uncover them in the preparatory stages.

The analyst/evaluator roles require a high level of skill in designing data collection tools, data collection itself, research methodologies and assessment techniques. They must have confidence that their data collection tools and strategies can uncover the relevant issues and generate data that are comprehensive and representative of the group of learners.

Both evaluators and analysts need to be skilled at formulating searching questions, and conducting interviews and focus groups. It is also important for these specialists to be aware of cultural attitudes that may influence the responses. In some cultures it is unacceptable to express opinions that differ from the most senior person in the group. In this situation a survey is more likely to provide more reliable data than a focus group. In some cultures respondents tend to choose the mid-point on a Likert-type scale survey irrespective of their real views.

Analyst/evaluators must be able to design surveys and questionnaires, and use basic statistical techniques to analyze the data collected. When using surveys to gather data globally, thought should be given as to whether translations are needed for any countries. If an English language survey is used worldwide, every effort should be made to communicate in unambiguous English, avoiding Western terms or jargon, and using simple sentence structures. When employing web-based surveys, the analyst/evaluator may need to partner with information technology specialists for a variety of tasks, such as ensuring that server space and technical support are available. This collaboration is particularly important in global data collection.

Planning and Analysis Skills

Identifying Learner and Environmental Characteristics. A clear statement of the target population, including the current skill level, is a key output of the analyst's work. In performance analysis and needs assessment the analyst must identify who needs the intervention, and report on learner characteristics to be taken into consideration by the design team. These typically include such demographics as cultural diversity, language fluency, learning preferences, variations in entry level knowledge across regions, level of motivation to change and availability of relevant technologies such as computers for web-based learning.

Analyst/evaluators must be able to recognize environmental factors that can influence the success of the intervention. The analyst identifies systemic issues that should be taken into account during the design and development phases. These same environmental factors may influence the attitudes of the learners toward the training, and negatively impact the transfer of learning to the work place. In highlighting work processes, structures or systemic factors that may undermine effective implementation the analyst is also looking ahead to the eventual diffusion of the instructional product. The evaluator uncovers environmental factors that undermine the post-implementation effects of the intervention. Examples include a lack of facilities or resources to deliver the training, lack of supervisor support for the intervention, an organizational culture that undermines the training, the need for job redesign, a lack of supporting processes, or the selection of under-qualified new hires. The analyst/evaluator should document these barriers as well as noting drivers or environmental factors that support the intervention.

Analyst/evaluators are concerned with the transfer of learning to the work environment, or the long-term impact of an intervention on the organization. These conclusions are dependent upon data from a variety of sources. They also build upon the initial needs assessment, especially when this process identified those factors the organization expected to be impacted by the training. When training courses have been presented globally, evaluation decisions must be reflective of the diverse environmental, social, cultural and physical influences that can impact both the delivery and the outcomes of training. The analyst/evaluator must be sensitive to the impact of cultural differences on learning, performance and long-term transfer. In many cases the impact of these systemic factors can not be anticipated or predicted because organizations lack a history of comprehensive training evaluation on a global basis. Similarly the effects of organizational culture must be taken into account. Organizational values and culture can undermine the instruction and account for the failure of training to effect changes in performance. The competent analyst/evaluator is mindful of these issues and attempts to assess their influence.

Conducting a Needs Assessment. Analysis is foundational to the entire instructional design process and is a critical facet of the analyst/evaluator's role. As a part of the needs assessment process, the analyst/evaluator must accurately describe the dimensions of current performance, identify the root causes of performance or attitudinal discrepancies, and recommend interventions to close the performance gap. The analyst must also prepare a cost benefit analysis for recommended solutions when required by a customer. It is especially critical that the analyst/evaluator reflects on data before finalizing recommendations. The analyst writes a performance analysis report after carefully reviewing all data and then proposes and advocates a range of solutions including non-instructional ones as appropriate. Even a variety of training interventions may be proposed for some performance gaps. Performance analysis and needs assessment of this caliber goes beyond confirming senior management's dictates or learners' requests because it is based on an in-depth assessment of the relationship between current performance and desired organizational outputs.

In evaluation efforts, data may suggest that certain instructional strategies have not been effective with certain groups of learners. The analyst/evaluator again must carefully consider the data before deciding whether to propose alternative strategies to address some of the training needs. This specialist's role demands reflection in all cases.

Design and Development Skills

Evaluating Interventions. Evaluation skills form the second major cluster of competence for the analyst/evaluator, but this work begins, not at the end of the project, but at an early stage of the design process. The analyst/evaluator plans both the evaluation and assessment strategies in partnership with others on the design team. Formative, summative, confirmative and impact evaluation strategies are developed at a macro level. At a micro level, the analyst/evaluator interacts with the designers and developers to select and sequence assessment techniques, construct and pilot test items, and advise on strategies for the assessment of learning throughout the training. At the conclusion of the evaluation process, the analyst/evaluator meets with stakeholders to present the findings and discuss recommendations. This group may include management, the design team, instructors, content specialists and developers. Organizational development specialists may also take on the stakeholder role if the evaluation identifies resistance to change.

Implementation and Management Skills

Working with Stakeholders. The competencies highlight the importance of promoting collaboration, partnerships and relationships among project stakeholders. The analyst/evaluator is dependent on the support and input of internal people to obtain the performance analysis data and insights needed to identify critical performance issues, root causes and a range of potential solutions. In some organizations performance analysis and needs assessment are regarded as time wasters and unnecessary. The skilled analyst/evaluator is able to identify the key stakeholders and persuade them, especially senior management, that analysis is imperative and a sound investment of time and money. The analyst/evaluator must also build collaborative relationships with potential subject matter experts during the data collection phase. Content experts often agree to act as project SMEs on the basis of relationships formed during the needs assessment phase.

Linking Recommendations to Strategic Goals. The analyst/evaluator's recommendations must always relate to the organization's strategic goals and the performance changes needed to achieve these goals. For the analyst/evaluator this is particularly important when findings do not support the prevailing view of a particular intervention. For example, evaluation data may show that a popular program is having no impact on work practice, or that the cost of the intervention outweighs the benefits. In such cases the findings may be discounted, challenged or even refuted by the instructional developers, the subject matter experts, the trainers, the primary customer, or the management. It is up to the analyst/evaluator to present persuasive arguments that will counteract such opinions.

The E-Learning Specialist

The E-learning specialist works in all phases of a project, but the majority of their focus is on the development of interventions. In large projects there may be several specialists fulfilling this role. The E-learning specialist's competencies relate to the following domains:

- Professional Foundations, with particular emphasis on communication skills as they relate to the use of instructional technology, and intellectual property rights;
- Planning and Analysis, with particular emphasis on identifying learner and environmental characteristics, and the use of technology;
- Design and Development, with particular emphasis on producing the interventions; and
- Implementation and Management, with particular emphasis on collaboration, and effective implementation.

Professional Foundation Skills

Communication. The majority of the communication competencies are important skills of the E-learning specialist. E-learning specialists require expertise in all facets of the design and development of technology-based learning including the use of color, interactivity, screen layout and motivating graphics. E-learning specialists must be skilled at reducing technical content to clear and unambiguous text for various delivery formats. They must also be able to use multimedia to visually stimulate the interest of the learner without compromising the instructional and learning requirements. Technology-based instruction may entertain users but its principal function is to contribute to learning and improved performance often in multi-cultural settings. In a sense these are all elements of communication.

The development of instructional content must take into account the relevant communication idiosyncrasies of the learners. For example, graphics and video examples must be appropriate to the context in which they will be used. A cultural informant is indispensable when developing materials for culturally diverse groups of learners.

On occasions the E-learning specialist will make presentations to various groups including management, the design team and subject matter experts. These presentations may showcase draft materials or demonstrate new instructional technologies in order to gain additional funding or other forms of support. Such presentations need to be well designed and delivered in order to positively influence the audience. E-learning specialists must be able to converse in both technical and non-technical language depending on the audience.

Intellectual Property. When developing or revising materials, the E-learning specialist must respect intellectual property. This is an increasingly complex task and one that can vary when dealing with technology. Care should be taken not to violate copyright when incorporating graphics, text, videoclips, web pages and other material into technology-based products. As with the generalist designer, E-learning specialists must be sensitive to potential legal consequences of their actions.

Planning and Analysis Skills

Learner and environmental characteristics. There are physical, social and cultural aspects of the learning environment that E-learning specialists should consider, and delivery strategy decisions should be based to some extent upon learners' characteristics. For example, certain occupational or cultural groups may be less likely to undertake self-directed learning, preferring interaction with others in classroom-based instruction. Older learners may lack confidence with computers and resist web-based courses.

E-learning specialists must take learner profile data into account. When the needs assessment does not include a comprehensive learner analysis in relation to technology-based learning preferences and computer skills, E-learning specialists must complete additional analysis of the target population. When learners come from different regions or ethnic groups, the E-learning specialist must be sensitive to cultural issues that may affect learning and performance. For example, certain cultural groups are uncomfortable with training that is not presented to the group by an "expert". When designing for a global audience designers are also obliged to consider the cultural impact of instructional materials, including sensitivity to the implications of using certain words, colors or symbols. The E-learning specialist may even have to consider translating materials into other languages.

E-learning specialists must also consider physical aspects of the learning environment. This is especially important for global instruction. For example, in some countries the unreliability of the telephone service makes web-based instruction difficult. Instructional interventions based on synchronous technologies for example, require a level of technical expertise and support that may not be available in some countries. Because of geographical differences an intervention may vary from region to region depending on the availability of the technology. If conditions are not appropriate for a project in some regions of the world, a less sophisticated delivery alternative must be selected.

Technology. E-learning specialists must be familiar with a wide range of established and emerging technologies, their advantages and drawbacks, and their effect on learner motivation and the learning process. This is obviously a fundamental area of competence for this specialist. While E-learning specialists use such skills during the planning and analysis phase expert performance is clearly dependent upon one's ability to remain current with the new technologies and relevant research and practice. They must know how to incorporate these new advancements to the development of technology-based instruction. This requires constant attention because of the pace of technological development. No other instructional design specialization is so demanding in this regard.

E-learning specialists must evaluate new technologies as they become available, assessing their potential learning applications and the capacity of the organizational infrastructure to support them in a single country or globally as necessary. They must also be able to project the cost and financial benefits to the organization of a proposed intervention, and provide cost comparisons with traditional delivery approaches. In some cases this is the only way to get a new (and usually expensive) instructional technology accepted by management. Many organizations' commitment to distance education is predicated upon the promise of a reduced training budget that would result from moving from centralized classroom training to a distributed learning approach.

Design and Development Skills

Instructional Materials Development. The principal work of the E-learning specialist is the development of new instructional products or the modification of existing materials. In many large organizations the development work is done in partnership with a content expert. Evaluation data from related courses should be used in conjunction with information provided by the needs assessment. Deciding which delivery medium to use will be influenced by knowledge about the shelf life of the content, the likelihood of policy changes, or the anticipation of frequent revisions to the instructional product.

The E-learning specialist must compare alternative solutions and provide a sound projection of costs and benefits of revising existing materials or building a new product. This is particularly important when technology-based instruction is proposed as a superior alternative to classroom instruction. The projection must not only show the cost savings over time but demonstrate that e-learning will lead to greater learning and performance.

One challenge facing E-learning specialists is the need to develop instructional materials that are content-rich, but also motivating and stimulating. Computer-based training that is little more than page turning on screen, or a CD ROM that relies on lengthy "talking head" videos are not an improvement on classroom based instruction, and will not engage learners.

It is also important for E-learning specialist to weigh alternative delivery solutions, and select that technology and strategy that accounts for desired learner outcomes, as well as the instructional context, learner motivation and assessment criteria. E-learning specialists may have to advise the customer that the requested solution (asynchronous delivery, web-based training, CD-ROM or some other "flavor of the month") is not the most effective delivery format when all elements of the situation are taken into account. They may also have to challenge the assumption that a training course is needed and suggest instead "just-in-time" information in the form of electronic job aids, for example. It is essential to revisit selected solutions if there are questions about the design, the delivery system, or the technology.

Implementation and Management Skills

Linking Efforts to Organizational Goals. All development work must be clearly linked to organizational strategy and the specific performance gaps that impact achievement of goals. It is the responsibility of this specialist to translate organizational priorities into interventions and instructional solutions. The E-learning specialist must ensure that interventions enhance organizational capability and are aligned with the specific needs initially expressed by the customer.

Collaboration. The E-learning specialist must be able to build and promote effective relationships to support the project. Collaborating with information technologists is imperative, especially in global projects with comparatively short cycle times. A strong partnership between the E-learning specialist and information technologists will ensure that both learners and instructors have the appropriate technology and software, as well as on-site support.

Effective implementation.   The E-learning specialist's active involvement in the "rollout" of a course is essential when a new technology is being introduced, or when there are technical support concerns. They also have a responsibility to monitor the delivery process, and make revisions to reflect changing circumstances within the organization or learner group.

The E-learning specialist can facilitate project implementation and management by documenting his or her work as a foundation for future efforts.   Cycle time and development costs can be significantly reduced by such data. Moreover, careful documentation at times makes it possible to reuse aspects of one project in another. An example of this would be reusing code in two computer based training projects.

Finally, E-learning specialists are responsible for designing the instructional management system that accompanies the product. Usually this system is embedded in the technical delivery system. The management system should capture data, such as grades, course completion, and other data required to meet government or legal regulations. Such data are especially critical in areas such as sexual harassment training for managers or training that relates to governmental and organizational regulations.

The Project Management Specialist

The Project Management specialist's competencies relate to the following domains:

- Professional Foundations, with particular emphasis on communication skills, and ethical and legal issues;
- Planning and Analysis; and
- Implementation and Management, with particular emphasis on project management, collaboration, and linking to organizational goals.

Professional Foundation Skills

Communication. In common with the other specialist roles, the instructional designer specializing in project management must demonstrate exemplary skill in several communication competencies. This specialist must be able to communicate with diverse groups of people within the organization, both individually and in groups. These groups may include senior managers or customers who have requested an update on the project, or finance personnel who are concerned about cost and budget issues. They may also include external consultants who are involved with aspects of the project, subject matter experts who have content issues to be discussed, or members of the project team who are often from fields other than instructional design. Project teams may include persons from different cultures with varying degrees of fluency in the primary language being used. The project manager must be sensitive to communication norms including preferences for written versus oral communication, translator needs, and dealing with team conflict.

The availability of meeting and networking technology has led to the widespread use of virtual project teams. Members of a virtual design team may be located in several different countries and regular meetings are held via conference call, Net Meeting or satellite hookup. While making global communication easier in many respects, technology has also exerted even more pressures on the personal communication skills of the project manager. Project management specialists now face the challenge of managing multi-located teams while communicating large amounts of information within short time frames. They may even need to facilitate team meetings across different time zones. For these reasons the project manager's written and spoken communications need to be of a very high standard.

Effective and efficient project team meetings do not just happen. Skilled project managers must know how to facilitate meetings with diverse groups within the organization. They must understand that meeting protocols vary according to region and attendees. They must determine who should attend project meetings and focus team discussions to quickly reach consensus. These skills all rely upon the use of active listening skills in all situations. Much of the project manager's work involves "keeping a finger on the pulse" by listening to problems, ideas, requests, new information and insights, and deciding on the appropriate course of action.

Ethical and Legal Issues. The project manager is responsible for monitoring the project in terms of ethical and legal implications. This includes working with designers and developers to check for copyright infringements in the reproduction of graphics, text and video clips, and taking care to safeguard the intellectual property of one's own organization. It is the project manager's responsibility to ensure contract personnel sign confidentiality agreements and clearly understand who owns the material developed or customized for the project. Other ethical and legal aspects monitored by the project manager include regulatory guidelines affecting the instructional intervention or its delivery and design decisions that run counter to organizational policies. They must also monitor instructional products that raise ethical or legal issues, such as the use of sexist or racist terminology.

Planning and Analysis Skills

Although none are central to the position, there are a variety of Planning and Analysis competencies that are related to the project manager's contributions to these phases of a design and development project. These include determining the scope of the program or curriculum, and ascertaining whether aspects of the corporate culture or organizational mission may influence the success of the project. The project manager, for example, works with the E-learning specialist to evaluate the capacity of the infrastructure in various parts of the organization to support the proposed delivery technology.

There are also supporting competencies that highlight the need for flexibility and a willingness to consider alternatives. The project manager must remain open to various solutions at different phases of the project, and reflect on problem situations and options before finalizing a decision about the preferred course of action. In troubleshooting a problem the project manager may be faced with several alternatives, each of which has a consequence for the success of the project. This competency requirement highlights the dynamic tension between the need to drive the project team to meet deadlines on the one hand, and the need to take time to reflect on problems and explore alternative solutions on the other.

Implementation and Management Skills

Effective Project Management. Project managers are responsible for controlling the scope of the project, particularly in terms of the logistics, and for controlling the resources, particularly in terms of personnel. The critical project scope competencies relate to writing the project proposal, and clarifying the project goals and deliverables, identifying material and human resources, and agreeing on the development time frame. These activities are done in collaboration with others, including the customer, the analyst/evaluator, the E-learning specialist and the manager of the entire instructional design group. Project managers may have some resources assigned to the project, but in other cases they will have to select team members.

Project managers may also be involved in recruiting external consultants. Project managers must know how to locate external specialists, negotiate fees, arrange contracts, and quickly integrate the external resources into the team. Project managers are also expected to be able to manage multiple projects simultaneously and troubleshoot problems as they arise. Throughout the life of the project, the project manager ensures that all aspects of the project are linked in to existing business or organizational processes such as record keeping, tracking, and other metrics.

As the key person managing the implementation phase of the project, this specialist provides whatever resources are required for effective implementation, and recommends plans for the organizational support of the program or intervention. Throughout the life of the project the project manager applies business skills to the management of the project. In particular, these involve the development of a budget, monitoring of expenditure, and the establishment of financial controls. At the end of a project, the project manager will debrief the team by reviewing the project history and discussing lessons learned. They may also document the project history and develop templates that can be used by future project managers.

Promoting Collaboration. Managing the project's resources, particularly the personnel, is arguably the most important aspect of the project manager's role. The competencies required by the project manager in this regard speak to the importance of establishing partnerships with stakeholders, clarifying their roles in the project, building strong relationships with the project team members, and adopting a collaborative working relationship with all who are involved in the project. In collaboration with others, the project manager typically assists in identifying subject matter experts and specialists for cross-functional teams. A principal role of the project manager is to promote and manage interactions among the team members. This can be demanding if the team is large, multi-located, or utilizes specialists from different groups within the organization who are not accustomed to working together. Most teams go through an initial period of establishing roles and norms, resolving differences about how certain tasks should be done and by whom, and dealing with differences of personality. The skilled project manager is able to guide the team through these potential conflicts, melding the team into a partnership of equals.

The project manager plans for the diffusion of the instructional or performance improvement products and partners with those involved in the implementation. In the initial phase of the implementation the project manager draws on his or her professional networks to gain support for pilot sites and participants. Without strong support from senior management, many projects falter at the diffusion stage. Collaboration with information technology specialists, as well as OD and HR groups is often essential to successful implementation as well.

The project manager must be skilled at maintaining the support of various stakeholder groups, particularly management, and for managing relations with internal and external customers. In each case, these supporting competencies require the ability to work with others as partners and to build relationships where the project manager has influence and credibility.

However, the project manager also continues to collaborate with members of the design team – even during the implementation phase. A key person involved at this point with the project manager is the analyst/evaluator since it is likely that the evaluation data will be used as an ongoing basis for revisions to the program or intervention.

Linking Efforts to Organizational Goals. Working with others on the team, the project manager continuously monitors the alignment of the project with the customer needs as well as the strategic plans of the organization. In a complex project with a long development cycle, the project can take on a life of its own thus losing its initial focus. It is therefore the responsibility of the project manager to maintain a clear and strong linkage between the project goals and the organizational requirements.

Conclusions

This chapter has examined the primary and supporting competencies of three emerging specializations within the instructional design field – the analyst/evaluator, the E-learning specialist, and the project manager. While it is more likely that these specializations will be found in large organizations, all instructional designers may find themselves in a specialist role on occasion. In such situations the ID competencies categorized by specialist roles can be a valuable resource.

Each specialist role has a number of competencies, some of which are primary and others that have a supporting role. Primary competencies are those which are most critical to the successful performance of the role. Supporting competencies, while not as critical, are nonetheless important to the effective performance of the specialist role.

Several of the competencies are common to each of the specialist roles discussed here. For example, each of the specialists requires a high level of communication skill, particularly the ability to adapt and tailor communication depending on the audience and situation. As the focus and scope of instructional design becomes more global in nature, the ability to communicate and collaborate across cultural boundaries is imperative. Likewise, designers have always had to take the characteristics of the learner and the learning environment into account. With training and performance interventions on a global scale, knowledge of cultural characteristics and their influence on the learning is now essential.

Another competency common to each specialist role is the need to link one's efforts to the strategic plans of the organization. This complements the trend for instructional designers to focus much more on the customers of the larger organization in which they work. At every point in the process, the design team needs to monitor the alignment of their activities with the outcomes desired by the customer. The analyst/evaluator also now seeks greater clarification of the performance problems in relation to anticipated organizational needs and goals. Continuously building these links with strategic goals and objectives ensures the maximum value from the resulting instructional products.

Instructional design is a dynamic and evolving field of practice. Given the rate of change in organizations, there is every reason to believe that further specializations will emerge in the practice of instructional design, and that the competencies required by the specialists described in this chapter will also change.

PART II

The IBSTPI ID Competencies: Validation

Chapter 6

The Competency Validation Research

The IBSTPI ID competencies are empirically-based. They are grounded in research, including:

- The research upon which the original IBSTPI ID competencies were based;
- The Atchison (1996) study that identified competencies of expert instructional designers;
- The Song (1998) study that sought to replicate the work of Atchison;
- IBSTPI board member focus groups;
- Validation by an international sample of instructional designers; and
- Review of all foundational data and final decision-making by the IBSTPI Board of Directors.

This chapter includes an overview of the formal research that was instrumental in the construction of these competencies \endash the Atchison and Song studies and the IBSTPI validation findings.

The Foundational Research

The Atchison Study

Purpose and Procedures. In 1992 Rowland argued that there had been little systematic investigation of what design practitioners actually did and that this impeded the field's ability to provide an accurate description of instructional design practice. Moreover, he suggested by this description that design practice should be approached by looking at designers with a range of expertise. Atchison's 1996 study was in many respects a response to Rowland's positions. Atchison sought to identify the professional competencies of expert instructional designers by examining the knowledge, skills, and attitudes they use to analyze instructional design problems, to implement design solutions, and to evaluate design effectiveness. He also examined the external and internal forces with an instructional setting that influenced this process. The ultimate goal of the research was to identify the competencies of expert instructional designers.

Atchison's study was qualitative in nature. His data were derived from long interviews of 15 expert designers working in four different work settings – higher education and vocational trade, business and industry, health care, and government. He used the critical incident method as a basis of generating discussion about the nature of their work. The data were analyzed to identify common themes.

Results. While all designers in the Atchison sample agreed that they need to know the core design skills and processes of instructional systems design, they spent an increasingly large amount of their time engaged in other activities. Using data from their interviews, Atchison identified multiple sets of exemplars which described expert instructional design competencies. Further analysis of these exemplars led to the creation of nine competency "themes" that the expert designers identified as critical to their practice. These themes were cast as designer roles. Ultimately, each of these roles was converted into a competency statement with supporting descriptors. They were:

1. *Demonstrates attributes of reflective practice.* This competency encompassed:
   - Using an intuitive sense of what was correct;
   - Transforming empathy for trainee needs into active learner engagement; and
   - Uncovering tacit knowledge of subject matter experts.

2. *Recognizes ethical issues in instructional design practice and is able to formulate an effective response.* This competency encompassed:
   - Identifying ethical dilemmas; and
   - Using ethical codes when responding.

3. *Demonstrates humanistic qualities.* This competency encompassed:
   - Expressing cultural competence; and
   - Showing a commitment to diversity issues;

4. *Demonstrates collaborative skills in instructional systems design.* This competency encompassed:
   - Building trust;
   - Coaching;
   - Monitoring natural work teams; and
   - Transforming clients into collaborators;

5. *Effectively advocates the legitimacy of instructional design practice to the client population.* This competency encompassed:
   - Using "people skills" to diffuse ISD innovations;
   - Keeping current in ISD research and theory; and
   - Applying theory to practice.

6. *Articulates and demonstrates an active commitment to maintaining the stability of evaluation systems in instructional design.* This competency encompassed:
   - Infusing front-end, formative and summative evaluation in all ID; and
   - Using diagnostic procedures to analyze instructional problems.

7. *Understands components of and effectively interacts with a business environment.* This competency encompassed:
   - Using knowledge of budgeting and cost and return analysis;
   - Collaborating in personnel management and development programs; and
   - Managing customer relations.

8. *Understands and effectively uses marketing principles to promotes instructional design services.* This competency encompassed:
   - Using market analysis principles;
   - Selling ISD; and
   - Using incentives to develop learner commitment.

9. *Is able to effectively diffuse innovative instructional design programs into various settings.* This competency encompassed:
   - Using effective consulting procedures;
   - Using knowledge of the "business ecology"; and
   - Presenting a "service orientation" to delivering instruction.

Application of these Findings. The Atchison competencies of expert designers were combined with the 1986 list of core ID competencies to form the first base list of revised competencies. While wording changed substantially, the vast majority of these competency areas receive the support of the larger sample of designers and remain in the final list.

The Song Study

Purpose and Procedures. Training and instructional design (ID) professionals perform in a wide variety of roles as they apply their competencies to the training and human resource development challenges facing their organizations. Concurrently, the call for accountability in all professions continues to increase, bringing with it a greater interest in credentialing and certification. ID competencies provide, especially those developed by IBSTPI, a practitioner-validated list of competencies needed by instructional designers.

Song's study addressed the issues of ID competency in the training and instructional design profession. As such, Song examined the perceptions of practicing professionals of to the 1986 IBSTPI ID competencies. In addition, Song utilized Atchison's (1996) "…nine competency themes that expert designers identified as critical to their practice" as a foundation for developing expert competencies to complete her survey instrument. Song had as her objective to determine if this expanded list of competencies was valid, and if an audience of practitioners could determine the level of expertise of ID competencies, and in doing so what would be the results.

Song's study was descriptive in method, and utilized the survey technique. The survey instrument was designed utilizing the 1986 ID IBSTPI competencies, and the expert themes identified by Atchison. The study evaluated the audience's perceptions of the level of complexity (Novice, Intermediate and Expert level) and validity of the competencies. Eighty surveys were mailed to members of the Minnesota chapter of ISPI and the St. Cloud Minnesota Chapter of ASTD.

Results. Nearly three fourths of the respondents worked in business, government and higher education settings with Master's degrees and experience in ID or related fields. The Song study re-established that the competencies derived from Atchison's expert themes were not only valid with a population of experienced professionals at the entry or mid-level, they rated them at the expert level with the exception of two which most respondents considered at the intermediate level. Of the 80 surveys, 33 responded with completed surveys and eight were returned incomplete. Thus the response rate was 41.25 percent for completed surveys and 51.25 for total replies. Eight respondents returned their surveys blank, stating that they were not familiar enough with the ID field or its significance to the profession to complete the survey.

Application of the Findings. The Song study was done subsequent to the Atchison study, thus providing the IBSTPI board with valuable data regarding the future revision process of the ID competencies. Furthermore, The Song study confirmed that some sort of rating levels for competencies, in terms of complexity of competencies, would have to be addressed in any effort at establishing a new set of IBSTPI competencies. Finally, the Song study provided evidence for the IBSTPI Board that some competency areas, such as communication and needs assessment, are perceived as essential for all instructional designers and trainers.

Organizations. Concurrently, the call for accountability in all professions continues to increase, bringing with it a greater interest in credentialing and certification. ID competencies provide, especially those developed by IBSTPI, a practitioner-validated list of competencies needed by instructional designers.

The Validation Research

Purpose and Scope of the Study

Once a base list of ID competencies and performance statements had been written, reviewed and revised to the extent that board approval was received, it was taken to the field for validation. There were four foci of this study:

- A determination of the level of criticality in the workplace of each competency and performance statement;
- A determination of whether the competencies and performances are reflective of novice designer activities, of experienced/expert designers, or of designers of all levels; and
- A determination that competency and performance statement language was consistent with that used in the workplace; and
- A determination that no critical areas of work had been ignored.

Ultimately, the aim of this research was to produce a final, validated set of competencies and performance statements for use in the profession. This was accomplished by accepting, rejecting, or modifying each of the newly revised competencies and performance statements, and adding new competencies or performances suggested by responding designers.

Procedures

Two survey instruments were constructed and field-tested. One measured designer perceptions of competency criticality and the second was used to determine the levels of expertise typically required on the job for the demonstration of each skill. Both instruments gathered reactions to each competency and each performance statement. In addition, key demographic data were identified on each instrument, including:

- Educational background;
- Gender and age;
- Geographical location;
- Primary design focus;
- Amount of work experience;
- Nature of current job (Percentage of time devoted to design, work setting); and
- Perceived level of expertise.

The two instruments were randomly distributed to subjects, so that each respondent completed only one survey. The data collection began in April 1998 and continued throughout 1998. Sample items from each instrument are shown in Figure 6.1.

Figure 6.1   Sample Items from Validation Data Collection Instruments

---

Criticality Survey

Below you will find the updated instructional designer competencies. The performances that contribute to the demonstration of each competency are listed (and indented) below each competency. Use a scale of 1-5 to indicate the level of *criticality* each of the competencies and their related performances have in the workplace.

1=None   2=Low   3= Moderate   4=High   5=Very High

Communicate effectively in visual, oral and written form.   1☐   2☐   3☐   4☐   5☐

Expertise Survey

Below you will find the updated instructional designer competencies. The performances that contribute to the demonstration of each competency are listed (and indented) below each competency. Use the scale of 1-3 to indicate the *level of expertise* possessed by designers who *typically* demonstrate the competencies and performances on their jobs.

1 = Demonstrated *typically* only by a *novice* designer – one who is trained, but has little if any work experience
2 = Demonstrated *typically* only by an *experienced/expert* designer – one who has a moderate to extensive amount of work experience and has developed considerable design skills
3 = Typically demonstrated by *both Novice and Experienced/Expert* Designers

We are not concerned at this point with the frequency with which a particular skill is used.

✓ *Check **one** box only.*

Communicate effectively in visual, oral, and written form.   1☐   2☐   3☐

A Description of the Respondents

Subjects were identified using the contacts of the members of the IBSTPI Board. This group is by design diverse, representing a variety of constituencies. They also represent a wide geographic range, including a cross-section of the United States, and Europe and Australia. Many Board members serve in leadership positions with other national professional organizations related to this discipline. Consequently, the Board has served as a valuable tool for identifying a diverse sample for this study.

The sample was not randomly selected. Consequently, the profile data cannot be assumed to be truly representative. Nonetheless, there is considerable

Table 6.1   A Personal Profile of Respondents to the ibstpi ID Competency Expertise and Criticality Surveys (N = 169)

Characteristic	Expertise Respondents		Criticality Respondents	
	N	%	N	%
Education				
• Bachelor's or less	22	26	21	25
• Master's & Ed.Spec	41	50	42	50
• Ed.D/Ph.D	20	24	19	23
Degree in ID or Related Field				
• No	31	38	31	38
• Yes	50	62	51	62
Gender				
• Male	40	50	40	49
• Female	40	50	42	51
Age				
• 20-40	37	45	36	43
• 41-50	29	35	33	40
• 51 & above	17	20	13	15
Level of ID Expertise				
• Low	13	16	6	7
• Moderate	17	21	22	27
• High	42	52	43	52
• Very High	9	11	12	14

diversity among the 175 respondents, 83 to the expertise survey and 92 to the criticality survey. While not all respondents chose to provide their profile data, it is nonetheless clear that the typical designer respondent was a person with a Master's degree in instructional design or a related field and in his or her 40's. Men and women were roughly equally represented and they characterized their own design expertise as high. These data are presented in Table 6.1.

The typical respondent worked in either the United States or Canada (most probably in the U.S.) in a business setting. His or her job was devoted, in the most part, to instructional design activities. The average work experience was nearly 11.5 years. The work profiles of respondents are shown in Table 6.2.

Table 6.2   A Work Profile of Respondents to the ibstpi ID Competency Expertise and Criticality Surveys   (N = 169)

Characteristic	Expertise Respondents		Criticality Respondents	
	N	%	N	%
Primary Region of Work				
• U.S./Canada	62	75	63	76
• Asia, Australia & New Zealand	9	10	8	9
• Europe & Other	12	14	12	15
Portion of Job with ID Focus				
• 20% or less	20	25	19	23
• 21-40%	9	11	11	13
• 41-60%	14	17	14	17
• 61-80%	20	25	15	18
• 81-100%	17	21	24	29
Type of Organization				
• Business/Industry	37	45	43	53
• Health Care	6	7	3	4
• Education	24	29	19	23
• Govt./Military	4	5	5	6
• Multiple Settings	12	14	9	11
• Other	0	0	2	2
Average Years of ID Work Experience				
• 11.37 Years for Expertise Respondents				
• 11.67 Years for Criticality Respondents				

Levels of Support

General Reactions. Even though there are varied reactions to this revised set of competencies and performance statements, on the whole respondents gave the list a high level of support by assigning high criticality ratings to the vast majority of the items using a 1-5 scale. (5 indicated a very high rating, 4 was high, 3 was moderate, 2 was low, and 1 indicated that the item was not critical at all.) Only one of the 23 competencies received a rating below 3.5, and that was 3.49. (This Professional foundation competency has been rounded-up and included in the 3.5 – 3.99 range in table 6.3.) The typical competency received a rating between 4.0 and 4.49. In general, there was a consistent pattern of the competency, a more general construct, receiving the highest rating and the more specific performance statements receiving equal or lower ratings. The typical performance statement received a rating between 3.5 and 4.49. Only one of the original 111 performance statements was rated below 3.0, and this item was rated 2.96. Tables 6.3 and 6.4 summarize the level of support for the competencies and performance statements clustered in the four competency domains.

Competency Ranking. Table 6.5 presents more specific results. The mean criticality rating, and the related variance, for each individual competency is shown. The competencies are then ranked (1 to 23) in terms of criticality.

Table 6.3 A Summary of the Level of Support for ibspti ID Competencies (N = 92)

Competency Domain	Criticality Rating Range						Total Across Competency Domains	
	4.5 – 5.0 Very High -		4.0 – 4.49 High +		3.5 – 3.99 High -			
	N	%	N	%	N	%	N	%
Professional Foundations	1	20	2	40	2	40	5	100
Planning & Analysis	1	14	5	71	1	14	7	99
Design & Development	1	17	5	83	0	0	6	100
Implement & Management	0	0	2	40	3	60	5	100
Total Across Competencies	3	13	14	61	6	26	23	100

Table 6.4   A Summary of the Level of Support for the Initial ibspti ID Performance Statements   (N = 92)

Competency Domain	Criticality Rating Range								Total Across Competency Domains	
	4.5 – 5.0 Very High -		4.0 – 4.49 High +		3.5 – 3.99 High -		3.49 & Below Moderate +			
	N	%	N	%	N	%	N	%	N	%
Professional Foundations	1	5	7	32	10	45	4	18	22	100
Planning & Analysis	1	3	17	59	11	38	0	0	29	100
Design & Development	2	7	19	61	10	32	0	0	31	100
Implement & Management	0	0	7	24	21	72	1	3	29	100
Total Across Performance Statements	4	4	50	45	52	47	5	5	111	100

The rankings do not appear to match the competency domains in any way. The top ranked competency (relating to effective communication) is in "Professional Foundations", but the second most critical competency (relating to needs assessment) is in "Planning and Analysis" and the third is in "Design and Development". One could only note that 4 of the 5 "Implementation and Management" competencies are ranked in the bottom half.

Table 6.5   A Summary of the Criticality & Expertise Ratings of the 2000 ibspti ID Competencies

Competency	N	Mean Criticality Rating (1-5; 5 high)	S.D	Criticality Rank	Level of Expertise
PROFESSIONAL FOUNDATIONS					
1 Communicate effectively in visual, oral and written form.	91	4.76	.56	1	Essential
2 Apply current research and theory to practice.	90	3.78	.76	21	Advanced
3 Update and improve one's skills and knowledge in instructional design and related fields.	89	4.25	.70	8	Essential
4 Apply basic research skills to design projects.	90	4.04	.85	17	Advanced
5 Identify and resolve ethical and legal implications of design and workplace environments.	90	3.49	1.03	23	Advanced

Continued

Competency	N	Mean Criticality Rating (1-5; 5 high)	S.D	Criticality Rank	Level of Expertise
PLANNING AND ANALYSIS					
6 Conduct a needs assessment.	89	4.65	.60	2	Essential
7 Design a curriculum or instructional program.	91	4.37	.74	4	Essential
8 Select and use a variety of techniques for determining instructional content.	91	4.25	.71	8	Essential
9 Identify and describe the target population characteristics.	91	4.18	.74	11	Essential
10 Analyze the characteristics of the environment.	91	3.88	.79	19	Essential
11 Analyze the characteristics of existing and emerging technologies and their use in an instructional environment.	91	4.09	.74	16	Essential
12 Reflect upon and study the elements of a situation before finalizing design solutions and strategies.	90	4.27	.80	6	Essential
DESIGN AND DEVELOPMENT					
13 Select, modify, or create a design and development model appropriate for a given project.	89	4.15	.89	13	Advanced
14 Select and use a variety of techniques to define and sequence the instructional content and strategies.	91	4.14	.80	14	Essential
15 Select or modify existing instructional materials.	91	4.18	.69	11	Essential
16 Develop instructional materials.	89	4.57	.69	3	Essential
17 Design instruction that reflects an understanding of the diversity of learners and groups of learners.	90	4.23	.69	10	Essential
18 Evaluate and assess instruction and its impact.	89	4.35	.76	5	Essential
IMPLEMENTATION AND MANAGEMENT					
19 Plan and monitor multiple instructional design projects.	91	4.10	.82	15	Advanced
20 Promote collaboration and partnerships among the key participants in a design project.	86	4.27	.79	6	Advanced
21 Apply business skills to managing instructional design.	90	3.98	.86	18	Advanced
22 Design instructional management systems.	87	3.61	.89	22	Advanced
23 Maintain the effective implementation of instructional products and programs.	91	3.82	.88	20	Essential

Levels of Expertise

General Reactions. Table 6.5 also presents summary results of the expertise ratings. There were no competencies that respondents indicated were typically demonstrated on the job by novice designers only. Eight of the competencies were associated with experienced or expert designers (listed as "advanced" in the table). The remaining 16 competencies were seen as more generic skills. In 1986, all IBSTPI competencies were labeled as core. There is no indication that this designation had data support at that time. Rather it appears to have been a matter of collective wisdom and conviction of the IBSTPI Board at that time.

It is noteworthy that 15 of the 23 competencies were given very high support by a consensus of respondents. Approximately two-thirds agreed that these skills were critical and there was a similar consensus that 10 of the 16 competencies should be considered essential and should be demonstrated by all designers regardless of level of expertise. There was a similar consensus with respect to 5 of the 7 advanced competencies.

Expertise Distribution Across Competency Domains. Today, the field of instructional design is more sophisticated and more complex than it was in 1986. Design teams, rather than individuals, commonly complete projects. Because of complexity of the job, few designers are fully competent in all aspects of the profession. Tables 6.6 and 6.7 are attempts to classify the levels of expertise needed by domains of competence.

Table 6.6   An Overview of Competency Domains by Level of Expertise

Level of Expertise	Mean Competency Criticality Rank	Frequency by Competency Domain								Total by Level of Expertise	
		Professional Foundations		Planning & Analysis		Design & Development		Implemention & Management			
		N	%	N	%	N	%	N	%	N	%
Essential	4.26	2	40	7	100	5	83	1	20	15	65
Advanced	3.92	3	60	0	0	1	17	4	80	8	35
TOTAL	4.14	5	100	7	100	6	100	5	100	23	100

Table 6.7 An Overview of Performance Statements by Level of Expertise

Level of Expertise	Frequency by Competency Domain								Total by Level of Expertise	
	Professional Foundations		Planning & Analysis		Design & Development		Implemention & Management			
	N	%	N	%	N	%	N	%	N	%
Essential	15	58	15	50	22	69	4	12	56	46
Advanced	11	42	15	50	10	31	30	68	66	54
TOTAL	26	100	31	100	32	100	34	100	122	100

There are patterns common to competencies found in Table 6.6 and other patterns found with respect to performance statements in Table 6.7. The key patterns pertaining to competency statements are:

- 65% of the competencies are essential to the work of all designers;
- The "Professional Foundations" are apparently not basic for all designers. There are expert as well as general foundations;
- The essential competencies of all designers seem to be clustered in "Planning & Analysis" and "Design & Development"; and
- The core set of advanced ID competencies is primarily clustered in the "Implementation & Management" and "Professional Foundations" domains.

An examination of the levels of expertise of the final 122 performance statements results in different conclusions. The primary ones are:

- There is a more balanced distribution of performance statements across the expertise continuum in the four different competency domains. Forty-six per cent of the performance statements are essential skills and 54% are advanced;
- Expert designers demonstrate the overwhelming two-thirds majority of performance statements in the "Implementation & Management" domain (68%); and
- The other three domains – Professional Foundations, Planning &

Analysis, and Design & Development continue to be more representative of essential skills, but there is, nonetheless, a substantial proportion of advanced skills included in these domains.

Implications for the Final ID Competencies

By and large, the validation research confirmed the ID competencies and performance statements. However, there was valuable input from the respondents that indeed did result in changes to the list. Most of these were wording changes that clarified the statements or emphasized aspects of the skill suggested by survey respondents. Seven competencies were reworded and 17 performance statements were reworded. However, 11 new performance statements were generated as a result of respondent input.

There were more changes in the Professional Foundations and the Implementation and Management domains than there were in Planning and Analysis or Design and Development. This is probably not surprising given the extensive research base and experience history in these two domains. These two domains consist primarily of essential skills, while the domains with more changes (Professional Foundations and Implementation and Management) contain more advanced skills.

The individual comments by survey respondents gave testimony to the changes that are taking place in instructional design. People spoke of technology demands, new techniques such as rapid prototyping and concurrent engineering, cognitive processing, learning organizations, and competency modeling. There were few responses that revealed a lack of knowledge of the topic at hand.

The most profound effects of the validation survey were on the performance statements. These new skills were suggested by multiple respondents many of whom wrote extensive statements describing their convictions.

When statements were reworded, the level of expertise determined through the research did not change. When new statements were added, however, there was a dilemma with respect to levels of expertise. This was resolved by attempting to adhere to the sense of the existing data. For example, since the communications competency and performance statements were overwhelmingly considered essential by the survey respondents, the new performance statement was also classified as essential. In some cases, decisions were not as clear. In these situations, the IBSTPI Board of Directors debated the issue and came to a decision based upon general consensus. One such example was the new performance statement on intellectual property rights. Even though the other parts of this competency array were deemed advanced by respondents, the Board assigned this to the essential cluster given the basic importance of the skill.

The new performance statements pertained to leading meetings, the ethical and legal dimension of design, working with subject matter experts, impact evaluation, project management, consultant management, developing design teams, data-based product revision, and obtaining organizational support. These additions in many cases tended to highlight key skills that were subsumed in more general terminology. In other cases, they were simply areas that had been neglected.

In summary, the research was an integral part of the competency development process. Just as the initial draft of the 2000 competencies was shaped by previous research, the final list of ID competencies and performance statements was built upon an even broader foundation of empirical data.

EPILOGUE

The new IBSTPI ID competencies are being introduced into a far different climate than those described by Foshay in the Preface. Today, many practitioners are anxiously awaiting the revised list to use in their departments. Academics have incorporated the competencies into design texts. Such a reception is due to a great extent because instructional design is now an established field and an important part of the education and training marketplace. It also reflects the growing importance of competency models in the field. The controversies surrounding the certification issue are still heated in many settings, and yet ID competencies are nonetheless useful even without the resolution of these debates.

The 2000 competencies differ from the 1986 set in a variety of ways. These include a presentation of competencies that:

- Cover a range of levels of design expertise;
- Emphasize design applications in the world of business;
- Attempt to provide a global orientation; and
- Reflect the changes in design practice, design theory, technology, and culture.

It would be naïve to presume that these 2000 ID competencies would be any more stable than those of 1986. One can assume that at some point in the future designers will see these as simplistic and dated as many now view the original set of competencies.

It is difficult to project the nature of the future changes other than anticipating a continuation of current trends. Technology will undoubtedly advance to an even greater extent. Work settings will probably become even more complex. Globalization will likely be seen as routine. However, other societal changes – changes less easy to predict – will take place that will impact the field of instructional design as they impact other disciplines and professions. The ID competencies of 2015 will reflect these new conditions.

There is a larger, as yet unanswered question, as to the extent to which the field needs competencies for more specialized roles. IBSTPI has produced instructor competencies and is currently revising its competencies for training managers. Are more focused sets of competencies and performance statements useful? Should specific competencies for on-line teaching be developed? Would evaluation or training facilitator's competencies be useful? Or distance educator competencies? These are questions that are being explored by IBSTPI. To a geat extent, the answers will come from the marketplace.

REFERENCES

Atchison, B.J. (1996). Roles and competencies of instructional design as identified by expert instructional designers. Unpublished doctoral dissertation. Detroit, MI: Wayne State University.

Briggs, L.J. (1977). *Instructional design: Principles and applications.* Englewood Cliffs, NJ: Educational Technology Publications.

Briggs, L.J.; Gustafson, K.L. & Tillman, M. H. (1991). *Instructional Design: Principles and Applications* (2nd ed.). Englewood Cliffs, NJ: Educational Technology Publications.

Browning, A.H; Bugbee, A.C. & Mullins, M.A. (Eds.). (1996). Certification: A NOCA handbook. The National Organization for Competency Assurance.

Carr-Chellman, A.; Cuyar, C. & Breman, J. (1998). User-design: A case application in healthcare training. *Educational Technology Research and Development,* 46(4), 97-114.

Clark, R. E. (1993). Media will never influence learning. *Educational Technology Research and Development,* 42(2), 21-30.

De Corte, E. & Weinert, F. (Eds.). (1996). *International encyclopedia of developmental and instructional psychology.* Oxford, UK: Pergamon Press.

Dick, W. (1987). A history of instructional design and its impact on educational psychology. In Glover, J.A. & Ronning, R.R. (Eds.), *Historical foundations of educational psychology* (pp. 183-202). New York: Plenum Press.

Dick, W. & Carey, L. (1978). *The systematic design of instruction.* Glenview, IL: Scott, Foresman and Company.

Dick, W. & Carey, L. (1996). *The systematic design of instruction.* (4th ed.). Glenview, IL: Scott, Foresman and Company.

Dick, W.; Watson, K. & Kaufman, R. (1981). Deriving competencies: Consensus versus model building. *Educational Researcher,* 10(10), 5-10.

Friedlander, P. (1996). Competency-driven, component-based curriculum architecture. *Performance and Instruction, 35*(2), 14-21.

Gilley, J.; Geis, G. & Seyfer, C. (1987). Let's talk certification: Questions and answers for the profession about the profession. *Performance and Instruction, 26*(2), xx-xx.

Grimstad Group (1995). Employment of system dynamics in modeling instructional design. In R. D. Tennyson & A. E. Barron (Eds.), *Automating instructional design: Computer-based development and delivery tools* (pp. 603-609). Berlin: Springer-Verlag.

Gustafson, K.L. & Branch, R.M. (1997). *Survey of instructional development models* (3rd ed.). Syracuse, NY: ERIC Clearinghouse on Information & Technology.

Industry Report, 1990. (October, 1990). *Training, 27*(10), 31-76.

Industry Report, 1999. (October, 1999). *Training, 36*(10), 37-80.

Instructional design competencies: The standards. (1986). Batavia, IL: International Board of Standards for Training, Performance and Instruction.

Jonassen, D. H. & Grabowski, B. L. (1993). *Handbook of individual differences: Learning and instruction.* Mahwah, NJ: Erlbaum.

Koschmann, T. (1996). *CSCL: Theory and practice of an emerging paradigm.* Mahwah, NJ: Erlbaum. (ED 400 783)

LeMaistre, C. (1998). What is an expert instructional designer? Evidence of expert performance during formative evaluation. *Educational Technology Research and Development 46*(3), 21-36.

Lucia, A.D. & Lepsinger, R. (1999). *The art and science of competency models: Pinpointing critical success factors in organizations.* San Francisco: Jossey-Bass/Pfeiffer.

Marrelli, A.F. (1998). An introduction to competency analysis and modeling. *Performance Improvement, 37*(5), 8-17.

Mayer, R.E. (1982). Learning. In Y.E. Mitzel (Ed.), *Encyclopedia of educational research* (pp. 1040-1058). New York: The Free Press.

McClelland, D.C. (1973). Testing for competence rather than for intelligence. *American Psychologist, 28*, 1-14.

McLagan, P.A. (May, 1997). Competencies: The next generation. *Training & Development*, 40-47.

Morrison, G.R.; Ross, S.M. & Kemp, J.E. (2001). *Designing effective instruction* (3rd ed.). New York: John Wiley & Sons, Inc.

Parry, S.B. (June, 1998). Just what is a competency? (And why should you care?). *Training, 35*(6), 58-64.

Perez, R.S. & Emery, C.D. (1995). Designer thinking: How novices and experts think about instructional design. *Performance Improvement Quarterly, 8*(3), 80-95.

Peterson, D. (1995). The reflective educator. *American Psychologist, 50*(12), 975-983.

Pieters, J.M. (1997). Training for human resources development in industrial and professional organizations. In Dijkstra, S. et al. (Eds.), *Instructional design: International perspectives. Volume 2: Solving instructional design problems* (pp. 315-340). Mahwah, NJ: Lawrence Erlbaum.

Richey, R.C. (1986). *The theoretical and conceptual bases of instructional design.* London: Kogan Page.

Richey, R.C. & Morrison, G.R. (2000). Instructional design in business and industry. In R.Reiser and J. Dempsey (Eds.), *Trends and Issues in Instructional Technology*. New York: Merrill, an imprint of Macmillan College Publishing Company.

Rosenberg, M.J.; Coscarelli, W.C. & Hutchison, C.S. (1999). The origins and evolution of the field. In H. D. Stolovitch & E.J. Keeps (Eds.), *Handbook of human performance technology* (2nd ed.) (pp. 24-46). San Francisco: Jossey-Bass/Pfeiffer.

Rothwell, W.J. & Kazanas, H.C. (1998). *Mastering the instructional design process: A systematic approach* (2nd ed.). San Francisco: Jossey-Bass Publishers.

Rowland, G. (1992). What do instructional designers actually do? An initial investigation of expert practice. *Performance Improvement Quarterly, 5*(2), 65-86.

Rowland, G. (1993). Designing and instructional design. *Educational Technology Research and Development, 41*(1), 79-91.

Schön, D. (1983). *The reflective practitioner: How professionals think in action.* New York: Basic Books.

Seels, B. (1989). The instructional design movement in educational technology. *Educational Technology, 29*(5), 11-15.

Seels, B. & Glasgow, Z. (1997). *Making Instructional Design Decisions* (2nd ed.). Columbus, OH: Merrill Publishing Company.

Seels, B. & Richey, R.C. (1994). *Instructional technology: The definition and domains of the field.* Washington, D.C: Association for Educational Communication and Technology.

Smith, P. L. & Ragan, T.J. (1999). *Instructional design* (2nd ed.). New York: Macmillan Publishing Company.

Song, J. (1998). An examination of the instructional design competencies written by the International Board of Standards for Training Performance and Instruction. Unpublished master's thesis. St. Cloud, MN: St. Cloud State University.

Spencer, L.M. & Spencer, S.M. (1993). *Competence at work: Models for superior performance.* New York: John Wiley & Sons, Inc.

Task Force on ID Certification (1981). Competencies for the instructional/training development professional. *Journal of Instructional Development, 5*(1), 14-15.

Tennyson, R. D.; Schott, F.; Seel, N. & Dijkstra, D. (Eds.). (1997). *Instructional design: International Perspectives, Volume 1: Theory, research, and models.* Mahwah, NJ: Erlbaum.

Young, J.I. & Van Mondfrans, A.P. (1972). Psychological implications of competency-based education. *Educational Technology, 12*(11), 15-18.

Visscher-Voerman, I.; Gustafson, K & Plomp, T. (1999). Educational design and development: An overview of paradigms. In J. van den Akker, et al. (Eds.), *Design approaches and tools in education and training* (pp.15-28). Dordrecht, The Netherlands: Kluwer Academic Publishers.

APPENDICES

The 1986 IBSTPI Instructional Design Competencies and Performance Statements

1 Determine projects that are appropriate for instructional design.
   a Discriminate between situations requiring instructional design solutions from those requiring other solutions (e.g., job redesign, organizational development), and decide if a project is appropriate for instructional design.
   b Judge the appropriateness and accuracy of instructional design project selection decisions.
   c State rationale for the decision or judgement.

2   Conduct a needs assessment.
    a   Develop a needs assessment/analysis plan.
    b   Conduct a needs assessment/analysis.
    c   Identify instructional problems.
    d   Judge the appropriateness, comprehensiveness and accuracy of given needs assessments/analysis plans and identified instructional problems.
    e   State rationale for the plan, interpretation or judgement.

3   Assess the relevant characteristics of learners/trainees.
    a   Select the learner/trainee characteristics that are appropriate for assessments.
    b   Determine methods for assessing these learner/trainee characteristics.
    c   Develop a profile of learner/trainee characteristics.
    d   Judge the appropriateness, comprehensiveness and adequacy of given selection of learner/trainee characteristics, the method for collecting data about those characteristics and the profile of learner characteristics.
    e   State rationale for the selection of learner/trainee characteristics, the method for collecting data about those characteristics, the profile of learner characteristics or judgement.

4   Analyze the characteristics of a setting.
    a   Determine and describe relevant resources and constraints of the development and delivery environments.
    b   Judge the accuracy, comprehensiveness and appropriateness of a setting analysis.
    c   State rationale for the selection of the resources and constraints of the development and delivery environments chosen for analysis or for the judgement made.

5   Perform job, task and/or content analysis.

   a   Select a procedure for analyzing the structural characteristics of a job, task or body of knowledge that is appropriate for that job, task or body of knowledge.

   b   Use a selected analysis procedure to identify the tasks and subtasks, cognitive processes and sequence of performance in a job, task or body of knowledge.

   c   State frequency, criticality and complexity or difficulty for each task or subtask.

   d   Identify the major concepts within the content, the relationships among concepts, the relationships (if any) with other content areas and critical attributes of key concepts.

   e   Judge the appropriateness, comprehensiveness and adequacy of a given methods selection and a given analysis.

   f   State rationale for the selection, analysis or judgement.

6   Write statements of performance objectives.

   a   State an objective in performance terms that reflects the intent of instruction.

   b   Judge weather objectives are stated in performance/behavioral terms; expressed as instructional goals, organizational goals Learner activities, teacher activities; or written in other styles.

   c   Judge the accuracy, comprehensiveness and appropriateness of statements of performance objectives in terms of the job, task or content analysis, and/or judgement/opinion of the client (e.g., subject matter expert, faculty).

   d   State rationale for the objectives written or for the judgement made.

7   Develop the performance measurements.
    a   Generate any of the following performance measures: criterion-referenced achievement tests, questionnaires, interviews, simulations, observations, performance checklists, product checklists.
    b   Judge the appropriateness, comprehensiveness and adequacy of given performance measurements.
    c   State rationale for the way the measurement instrument is constructed or for the judgement made.

8   Sequence the performance objectives.
    a   State rules for sequencing performance objectives appropriate to a given situation.
    b   Sequence the objectives by applying the rules.
    c   Judge the accuracy, comprehensiveness and appropriateness of a given sequence of performance objectives.
    d   State rationale for the rules, sequence or judgement.

9   Specify the instructional strategies.
    a   Specify the instructional strategy (techniques, media and settings) to be used in the instructional system being developed.
    b   Judge the appropriateness of a specified instructional strategy for a given instructional system.
    c   State rationale for the specification or the judgement.

10 Design the instructional materials.
    a   Write instructional materials for learners (and/or instructors and/or media producers) in a selected medium.
    b   Judge the accuracy, completeness and appropriateness of existing instructional materials in a selected medium.
    c   State rationale for judging existing materials or for the way newly developed materials are written.

11 Evaluate the instruction/training.
    a Develop a formative evaluation plan.
    b Conduct a formative evaluation.
    c Generate specifications for revision of training based on evaluation feedback.
    d Judge the appropriateness, comprehensiveness and adequacy of given formative evaluation plans and revision specifications.
    e State rationale for the formative evaluation plan, revision specifications or judgements.

12 Design the instructional management system.
    a Design an instructional management system for a course, training package or workshop.
    b Judge the appropriateness, comprehensiveness and adequacy of a given instructional management system.
    c State rationale for the design or judgement.

13 Plan and monitor instructional design projects.
    a Develop a project management plan for an instructional design project.
    b Monitor an instructional design project for adherence to the project management plan.
    c Judge the appropriateness and comprehensiveness of a given project plan.
    d State rationale for the project plan or the judgement of it.

14 Communicate effectively in visual, oral and written form.
    a Communicate effectively in visual, oral and written form.

15 Interact effectively with other people.

    a   Establish rapport with individuals and groups.

    b   State the purpose and / or agenda of an interaction.

    c   Ask questions of individuals or groups.

    d   Explain information to individuals or groups.

    e   Listen to individuals or groups.

    f   Deal with friction among members of a group.

    g   Deal with resistance from an individual or groups.

    h   Keep an individual or groups on track.

    i   Obtain commitment from an individual or group.

    j   Select and tailor appropriate behaviors for specific interactions with other people.

    k   Judge the appropriateness and effectiveness of behaviors used in specific interactions with other people.

    l   State rationale for the selection and tailoring of appropriate behaviors for specific interactions with other people.

16 Promote the use of instructional design.

    a   Specify ways the training unit and organization can be made aware of current professional instructional design practices.

    b   State rationale for diffusion tactics

Glossary of IBSTPI Instructional Design Terms

With J. Michael Spector

Advanced capabilities – those knowledge, skills, and judgements demonstrated by experienced and expert designers. Applied to both competencies and performance statements.

Assessment – a measure of individual learning for various purposes, including a determination of readiness for learning, monitoring progress, and measuring achievement after instruction.

Benchmarking – the process of comparing curricula and other organizational information with best practice programs.

Business case – the business-related reason for which a training or performance intervention is needed.

Consultant – an individual or organization retained to work on a project because of specific expertise. May be internal to one's organization or external. Related Term: Contractor.

Competency – a knowledge, skill or attitude that enables one to effectively perform the activities of a given occupation or function to the standards expected in employment. Related Term: Competence.

Confirmative evaluation – the process of determining whether over time learners have maintained their level of competence, the instructional materials remain effective, and the organizational problems have been solved. Confirmative evaluation occurs after formative and summative evaluation (Seels and Richey, 1994, p.126).

Cost benefit analysis – a comparison of the economic benefits of the program to the actual and opportunity costs of the program. Related Term: Trade-off analysis.

Criticality – the extent to which a behavior or activity is viewed as essential to a designer's job.

Cross-functional teams – teams in which instructional designers work with specialists from other fields, such as organizational development, and multi-media development and engineering.

Curriculum – a large body of organized and sequential instruction, consisting of programs and courses. May also refer to the aggregate of modules or courses directed toward a common goal of a given organization, or a collection of required readings.

Customer – a person or organization for which a service is performed. May be internal to one's organization or external. Related Term: Client.

Delivery system – a means of organizing, presenting, or distributing instruction, typically employing a variety of media, methods and materials.

Domain – a cluster of related competencies. Other uses: a subject matter area.

E-learning specialist – a person with expertise in the delivery of content via all electronic media, including the Internet, intranets, satellite broadcast, multi-media, audio/video tape, interactive TV, and CD-ROM.

Emerging technologies – new techniques, tools and equipment used in designing or delivering instruction, including virtual reality, electronic performance support systems, and multi-user object-oriented domains.

Essential capabilities – those knowledge, skills, and judgements that all designers should be able to demonstrate. Applied to both competencies and performance statements.

Evaluation – the process of determining the adequacy, value, outcomes and impact of instruction and learning (adapted from Seels and Richey, 1994, p.128).

Expert instructional designer – a person with a foundation of formal training in the field, typically a graduate degree, substantial work experience, and the facility to anticipate design problems and quickly identify effective design solutions. Related Term: Experienced instructional designer.

Expertise– the level of knowledge and experience demonstrated by designers who are typically categorized as either novice, experienced, or expert.

Formative evaluation – gathering information on the adequacy of an instructional product or program and using this information as a basis for further development (Seels and Richey, 1994, p.128).

Fundamental research skills – those skills which are basic to scientific investigation, including the design of exploratory studies and field tests, instrument design and data collection techniques, and the interpretation and analysis of qualitative and quantitative data.

Individualization – tailoring instruction to meet the abilities, knowledge, skills, interests, motivation and goals of individual learners.

Instruction – a planned process that facilitates learning.

Instructional context – the physical and psychological environment in which instruction is delivered or in which transfer occurs. Related Term: Learning environment.

Instructional design – systematic instructional planning including needs assessment, development, evaluation, implementation and maintenance of materials and programs. Related Term: Instructional systems design.

Instructional design theory – a set of scientific principles relating to instructional methods, learner characteristics, learning environments, and outcomes. Typically derived from or tested by empirical research.

Instructional goal – a general statement of learner outcomes, related to an identified problem and needs assessment, and achievable through instruction (Dick and Carey, 1996, p. 23).

Instructional objective – a detailed description of what learners will be able to do having completed a unit of instruction (Dick and Carey, 1996, p. 119). Related Terms: Learning outcome, behavioral objective, performance objective.

Instructional products – content-related items such as books, job aids, student and instructor guides, and web pages.

Instructional strategy – a general approach to selecting and sequencing learning activities. Related Term: Teaching methods.

Instructional Systems Design – an organized procedure for developing instructional materials, programs, or curricula; includes the steps of analyzing, designing, developing, implementing, and evaluating. Related Terms: Instructional design, instructional systems development.

Intellectual property – the technological or process knowledge and capabilities that an organization or an individual has developed. Typically protected by copyright.

Learner profile data – descriptions of the learner characteristics pertinent to instruction, including factors such as age, skill level, education and work experience. Related Term: Target population characteristics.

Learning – a relatively stable change in knowledge or behavior as a result of experience (Mayer, 1982, p. 1040).

Learning style – an individual's preferred means of acquiring knowledge and skills. Related Terms: Cognitive style, multiple intelligences.

Media – the means by which instruction is presented to the learner. Typically classified in terms of the perceptual channels employed, such as visual or auditory media.

Message – a meaningful unit of communication that may take alternative forms, including written, visual or oral. Messages may be instructional, informational, or motivational.

Multi-media – the integration of various forms of media for instructional purposes. Typically involving computer graphics, animation, video, sound, and text.

Needs assessment – a systematic process for determining goals, identifying discrepancies between optimal and actual performance, and establishing priorities for action. (Briggs, 1977, p.xxiv). Related Terms: Training needs assessment, needs analysis, front-end analysis, task and subject matter analysis.

Novice instructional designer – a person who has received basic training and education in instructional design fundamentals, but has little or no actual on-the-job work experience.

Organizational mission – a description of the organization's purpose, values, strategic position, and long-term goals.

Organizational philosophy - a description of an organization's values and beliefs with regard to how it intends to act and interact in its environment.

Organizational values – a stable set of long-term aspirations and actions that the organization uses to make strategic choices. Related Term: Corporate culture.

Performance improvement – the process of designing or selecting interventions directed toward a change in behavior, typically on the job. Related Terms: Performance technology, human performance technology.

Performance statement – a detailed explanation of activities comprising a competency statement.

Professional activities – conduct which enhances the skill and knowledge of the instructional design practitioner, including attending professional association meetings and conference, reading relevant texts, or networking with other practitioners.

Program – a unit of instruction consisting of two or more courses, modules, workshops, seminars and the like. Related Term: Curriculum.

Project information systems – organized processes and databases used to manage projects and resources.

Reliability – the degree to which items consistently yield the same or comparable results.

Stakeholders – people with a vested interest in project outcomes.

Strategic plan – a process for allocating resources to achieve long-range organizational goals

Subject matter expert – a content specialist who advises or assists the designer. Related Terms: SME, content expert.

Summative evaluation – systematically gathering information on the adequacy and outcomes of an instructional intervention and using this information to make decisions about utilization (Seels and Richey, 1994, p.134).

Tactical goals – statements that specify short-term actions required to achieve an organization's strategic goals.

Target population – those persons for whom an instructional intervention is intended. Related Terms: The learners, the learner group.

Transfer – the application of knowledge and skills acquired in training to another environment, typically a work setting.

Validation – the process of determining the extent to which competencies and performance statements are supported by the profession.

Validity – the degree to which items measure what they are intended to measure. Related Term: Valid test items.

Visuals – graphics or teaching materials that pictorially describe ideas or convey meaning, including items such as overhead transparencies, screen graphics, or icons. Related Term: Visual aids.

Bibliography of Instructional Design References

General ID Books

Briggs, L.J.; Gustafson, K.L.; and Tillman, M. H. (1991). *Instructional Design: Principles and Applications* (2nd ed.). Englewood Cliffs, NJ: Educational Technology Publications.

Dick, W. and Carey, L. (1996). *The systematic design of instruction.* (4th ed.). Glenview, IL: Scott, Foresman and Company.

Gagné, R.M., Briggs, L.J. & Wager, W.W. (1992). *Principles of instructional design* (4th ed.). New York: Holt, Rinehart and Winston, Inc.

Gagné, R.M. & Medsker, K.L. (1996). *The conditions of learning: Training applications.* Fort Worth, TX: Harcourt Brace College Publishers.

Morrison, G.R.; Ross, S.M.; & Kemp, J.E. (2000). *Designing effective instruction* (3rd ed.). New York: Merrill Publishing.

Reiser, R.A. & Dick, W. (1996). *Instructional planning: A guide for teachers* (2nd ed.). Boston: Allyn and Bacon.

Romiszowski, A.J. (1981). *Designing instructional systems: Decision making in course planning and curriculum design.* London: Kogan Page.

Rothwell, W.J. & Kazanas, H.C. (1998). *Mastering the instructional design process: A systematic approach* (2nd ed.). San Francisco: Jossey-Bass Publishers.

Seels, B. & Glasgow, Z. (1997). *Making Instructional Design Decisions* (2nd ed.). Columbus, OH: Merrill Publishing Company._

Smith, P. L. & Ragan, T.J. (1999). *Instructional design* (2nd ed.). New York: Macmillan Publishing Company

ID Research and Theory

Bonner, J. (1988). Implications of cognitive theory for instructional design: Revisited. *Educational Communications and Technology Journal, 36*(1), 3-14.

Clark, R.E. (1994). Media will never influence learning. *Educational Technology Research and Development, 42*(2), 21-30._

Duffy, T.M. & Jonassen, D.H. (Eds.). (1992). *Constructivism and the technology of instruction: A conversation.* Hillsdale, NJ: Lawrence Erlbaum Associates, Publishers. (ED 364 198)

Gagné, R.M. (1985). *The conditions of learning and theory of instruction* (4th ed.). New York: Holt, Rinehart and Winston, Inc.

Gagné, R.M. (1989). *Studies of learning: 50 years of research.* Tallahassee, FL: Florida State University Learning Systems Institute.

Hlynka, D. (1991). Post-modern excursions into educational technology. *Educational technology, 31*(6), 27-30.

Jonassen, D.H. & Tessmer, M. (1996/1997). An outcomes-based taxonomy for instructional systems design, evaluation, and research. *Training Research Journal, 2,* pp. 11-46.

Land, S.M. & Hannafin, M.J. (1996). A conceptual framework for the development of theories-in-action with open-ended learning environments. *Educational Technology Research and Development, 44*(3), 37-53.

Martin, B.L. and Briggs, L.J. (1986). *The affective and cognitive domains: Integration for instruction and research.* Englewood Cliffs, NJ: Educational Technology Publications.

Merrill, M.D. (1983). Component display theory. In C.M. Reigeluth (Ed.), *Instructional design theories and models: An overview of their current status* (pp. 279-334). Hillsdale, NJ: Lawrence Erlbaum Associates.

Merrill, M.D. (1994). *Instructional design theory.* Englewood Cliffs, NJ: Educational Technology Publications.

Merrill, M.D.; Tennyson, R.D. & Posey, L.O. (1992). *Teaching concepts: An instructional design guide* (2nd ed.). Englewood Cliffs, NJ: Educational Technology Publications.

Perez, R.S. & Emery, C.D. (1995). Designer thinking: How novices and experts think about instructional design. *Performance Improvement Quarterly, 8*(3), 80-95.

Reigeluth, C.M. (Ed.). (1983). *Instructional-design theories and models: An overview of their current status.* Hillsdale, NJ: Lawrence Erlbaum Associates.

Reigeluth, C.M. & Stein, S.S. (1983). The elaboration theory of instruction. In C.M. Reigeluth (Ed.), *Instructional design theories and models: An overview of their current status* (pp. 335-379). Hillsdale, NJ: Lawrence Erlbaum Associates.

Richey, R.C. (1986). *The theoretical and conceptual bases of instructional design.* London: Kogan Page.

Richey, R.C. (1992). *Designing instruction for the adult learner: Systemic theory and practice for employee training.* London: Kogan Page.

Richey, R.C. (1993). Instructional design theory and a changing field. *Educational Technology, 33*(2), 16-21.

Rowland, G. (1992). What do instructional designers actually do? An initial investigation of expert practice. *Performance Improvement Quarterly, 5*(2), 65-86.

Rowland, G. (1993). Designing and instructional design. *Educational Technology Research and Development, 41*(1), 79-91.

Spector, J.M.; Polson, M.C. & Muraida, D.J. (Eds.) (1993) *Automating insructional design: Concepts and issues.* Englewood Cliffs, NJ: Educational Technology Publications.

Tennyson, R.D. (1995). The impact of the cognitive science movement on instructional design fundamentals. In B. Seels (Ed.), *Instructional design fundamentals: A reconsideration.* (pp. 109-132). Englewood Cliffs, NJ: Educational Technology Publications.

West, C.K.; Farmer, J.A. & Wolff, P.M. (1991). *Instructional design: Implications from cognitive science.* Englewood Cliffs, NJ: Prentice Hall.

Wilson, B.G. (Ed.) (1996). *Constructivist learning environments: Case studies in instructional design.* Englewood Cliffs, NJ: Educational Technology Publications.

Wilson, B. & Cole, P. (1991). A review of cognitive teaching models. *Educational Technology Research and Development, 39*(4), 47-64.

Wilson, B. and Cole, P. (1992). A critical review of elaboration theory. *Educational Technology Research and Development, 40*(3), 63-79.

Winn, W. (1993). Instructional design and situated learning: Paradox or partnership? *Educational Technology, 33*(3), 16-11.

ID Models, Tools and Techniques

Andrews, D.H. & Goodson, L.A. (1980). A comparative analysis of models of instructional design. *Journal of Instructional Development, 3*(4), 2-16.

Dick, W. (1993). Enhanced ISD: A response to changing environments for learning and performance. *Educational Technology, 33*(2), 12-16.

Dick, W. (1995). Instructional design and creativity: A response to the critics. *Educational Technology, 35*(4), 5-11.

Dick, W. (1996). The Dick and Carey model: Will it survive the decade? *Educational Technology Research and Development, 44*(3), 55-63.

Gustafson, K.L. & Branch, R.M. (1997). *Survey of instructional development models* (3rd Ed.). Syracuse, NY: ERIC Clearinghouse on Information Resources, Syracuse University.

Hiemstra, R. & Sisco, B. (1990). *Individualizing instruction: Making learning personal, empowering, and successful.* San Francisco: Jossey-Bass.

Jonassen, D.H.; Grabinger, R.S. & Harris, N.D.C. (1991). Analyzing and selecting instructional strategies and tactics. *Performance Improvement Quarterly,* 4(2), 77-97.

Keller, J.M. (1987). The systematic process of motivational design. *Performance and Instruction, 26*(10), 1-8.

Leshin, C; Pollock, J. & Reigeluth, C.M. (1992). *Instructional design strategies and tactics.* Englewood Cliffs, NJ: Educational Technology Publications.

Muraida, D.J. & Spector, J.M. (1993). The advanced instructional design advisor. *Instructional Science, 21*(4), 239-253.

Reigeluth, C. M. (Ed.). (1999). *Instructional-design theories and models: A new paradigm of instructional theory, vol. 2.* Mahwah, NJ: Lawrence Erlbaum Associates.

Richey, R.C. (1995). Trends in instructional design: Emerging theory-based models. *Performance Improvement Quarterly,* 8(3), 96-110.

Tessmer, M. & Wedman, J.F. (1990). A layers of necessity instructional development model. *Educational technology research and development, 38*(2), 77-85.

Tessmer, M. & Wedman, J.F. (1995). Context-sensitive instructional design models: A response to design theory, practice, and criticism. *Performance Improvement Quarterly,* 8(3), 38-55.

Tripp, S. & Bichelmeyer, B. (1990). Rapid Prototyping: An alternative instructional design strategy. *Educational Technology Research and Development, 38*(1), 31-44.

Wedman, J. & Tessmer, M. (1993). Instructional designers' decisions and priorities: A survey of design practice. *Performance Improvement Quarterly,* 6(2), 43-57.

Wilson, B.G. & Jonassen, D.H. (1990/91). Automated instructional systems design: A review of prototype systems. *Journal of Artificial Intelligence in Education, 2*(2), 17-xx.

Professional Foundations

Dean, P. (1992). The relevance of standards and ethics for the human performance profession. In H.D. Stolovitch & E. J. Keeps (Eds.), *Handbook of human performance technology: A comprehensive guide for analyzing and solving performance problems in organizations* (pp. 698-712). San Francisco: Jossey-Bass.

Dean, P. (1993). A selected review of the underpinnings of ethics for human performance technology professionals, Part 1: Key ethical theories and research. *Performance Improvement Quarterly,* 6(4), 3-32.

Driscoll, M. (1993). *Psychology of learning for instruction.* Needham Heights: MA: Allyn and Bacon.

Ely, D. P. (1996). *Trends in educational technology.* Syracuse, NY: ERIC Clearinghouse on Information and Technology, Syracuse University.

Eyres, P. (1992) Legal implications of Human Performance Technology. In H.D. Stolovitch and E. J. Keeps (Eds.), *Handbook of human performance technology: A comprehensive guide for analyzing and solving performance problems in organizations* (pp. 586-601). San Francisco: Jossey-Bass.

Gilbert, T. F. (1996). *Human Competence: Engineering Worthy Performance.* New York: McGraw-Hill.

Harris, P.R. & Moran, R.T. (1996). *Managing cultural differences.* (4th ed.). Houston, TX: Gulf Publishing.

Hoecklin, L. (1995). *Managing cultural differences: Strategies for competitive advantage.* Addison-Wesley Publishers Ltd.

Jonassen, D. H. (Ed.). (1996). *Handbook of research for educational communications and technology.* New York: Macmillan.

McLagan, P. & Krembs, P. (1995). *On-the-level: Performance communication that works.* San Francisco: Berrett-Koehler Publishers, Inc.

Robinson, D.G. & Robinson, J. C. (Eds.). (1998). *Moving from training to performance: A practical guide book.* San Francisco: Berrett-Koehler and American Society for Training and Development.

Seels, B. B. & Richey, R. C. (1994). *Instructional technology: The definition and domains of the field.* Washington, DC: Association for Educational Communications and Technology.

Senge, P.M. (1990). *The fifth discipline: The art and practice of the learning organization.* New York: Doubleday.

Stolovitch, H. D. & Keeps, E. J. (Eds.), (1999). *Handbook of human performance technology* (2nd ed.). San Francisco: Jossey-Bass/Pfeiffer.

Strauss, A. & Corbin, J. (1990). *Basics of qualitative research.* Thousand Oaks, CA: Sage.

Swanson, R.A. & Holton, E.F. (Eds.). (1997). *Human resource development research handbook: Linking research and practice.* San Francisco: Berrett-Koehler Publishers, Inc.

Westgaard, O. (1992). Standards and ethics for practitioners. In H.D. Stolovitch & E. J. Keeps (Eds.), *Handbook of human performance technology: A comprehensive guide for analyzing and solving performance problems in organizations* (pp. 576-585). San Francisco: Jossey-Bass.

Planning and Analysis

Edwards, J.E.; Thomas, M.D.; Rosenfield, P. & Booth-Kewley, S. (1997). *How to conduct organizational surveys: A step-by-step guide.* Thousand Oaks, CA: Sage Publications.

Foshay, W.R. (1983). Alternative methods of task analysis. *Journal of Instructional Development, 6*(4), 2-9.

Fulop, M.; Loop-Bartick, K. & Rossett, A. (1997). Using the World Wide Web to conduct a needs assessment. *Performance Improvement, 36*(6), 22-27.

Kaufman, R.; Rojas, A. M. & Mayer, H. (1993). *Needs assessment: A user's guide.* Englewood Cliffs, NJ: Educational Technology Publications.

Robinson, D.G. & Robinson, J. C. (1995). *Performance consulting.* San Francisco: Berrett-Koehler.

Rossett, A. (1987). *Training needs assessment.* Englewood Cliffs, NJ: Educational Technology Publications.

Rossett, A. (1999). *First things fast: A handbook for performance analysis.* San Francisco: Jossey-Bass Pfeiffer.

Ryder, J.M. & Redding, R.E. (1993). Integrating cognitive task analysis into instructional systems development. *Educational Technology Research and Development, 41*(2), 75-96.

Sleezer, C. M. (1993). Training needs assessment at work: A dynamic process. *Human Resource Development Quarterly, 4*(3), 247-264.

Tessmer, M. (1990). Environment analysis: A neglected stage of instructional design. *Educational Technology Research and Development, 38*(1), 55-64.

Tessmer, M.& Harris, D. (1992). *Analysing the instructional setting: Environmental analysis.* London/Bristol, PA: Kogan Page/Taylor and Francis.

Tessmer, M. & Richey, R.C. (1997) The role of context in learning and instructional design. *Educational Technology Research and Development, 45*(2), 85-115.

Wolfe, P.; Wetzel, M.; Harris, G.; Mazour, T. & Riplinger, J. (1991). *Job task analysis: Guide to good practice.* Englewood Cliffs, NJ: Educational Technology Publications.

Zemke, R. (1998). How to do a needs assessment when you think you don't have time. *Training, 35*(3), 38-44.

Multimedia and E-Learning

Brown, L. A. (1996). *Designing and developing electronic performance support systems.* Woburn, MA: Butterworth-Heinemann.

Clark, R.E. (1994). Media will never influence learning. *Educational Technology Research and Development, 42*(2), 21-30.

Cyrs, T. E. (1997). *Teaching at a distance with the merging technologies: An instructional systems approach.* Las Cruces, NM: Center for Educational Development, New Mexico State University.

Dillon, A.; Rouet, J.; Levonen, J. T. & Spiro, R. J. (Eds.) (1996). *Hypertext and cognition.* Mahwah, NJ: Lawrence Erlbaum Associates.

Driscoll, M. (1998). *Web-based training: Using technology to design adult learning experiences.* San Francisco: Jossey-Bass.

Fleming, M.L. & Levie, W.H. (1993). *Instructional message design* (2nd ed.). Englewood Cliffs, NJ: Educational Technology Publications.

Gayeski, D. M. (1993). *Multimedia for learning: Development, application, evaluation.* Englewood Cliffs, NJ: Educational Technology Publications.

Gery, G. (1991). *Electronic performance support systems.* Boston, MA: Weingarten Publishers.

Gibbons, A. S. & Fairweather, P. G. (1998). *Computer-based instruction: Design and development.* Englewood Cliffs, NJ: Educational Technology Publications.

Jonassen, D. H.; Peck, K. L. & Wilson, B. G. (1999). *Learning with technology: A constructivist perspective.* Upper Saddle River, NJ: Merrill.

Khan, B. H. (Ed.) (1997). *Web-based instruction.* Englewood Cliffs, NJ: Educational Technology Publications.

Newby, T. J.; Stepich, D. A.; Lehman, J. D. & Russell, J. D. (1996). *Instructional technology for teaching and learning: Designing instruction, integrating computers, and using media.* Englewood Cliffs, NJ: Merrill.

Pallesen, P. J.; Haley, P.; Jones, E. S.; Moore, B.; Widlake, D. E. & Medsker, K. L. (1999). Electronic delivery systems. *Performance Improvement Quarterly,* 12(4), 7-32.

Piskurich, G.M. (1993). *Self-directed learning: A practical guide to design, development, and implementation.* San Francisco: Jossey-Bass.

Romiszowski, A.J. (1988). *The selection and use of instructional media: For improved classroom teaching and for interactive, individualized instruction* (2nd ed.). London: Kogan Page.

Rossett, A. & Barnett, J. (1996). Designing under the influence: Instructional design for multimedia training. *Training,* 33(12), 33-43.

Rumble, G. (1999). Cost analysis of distance learning. *Performance Improvement Quarterly,* 12(2), 122-137.

Wileman, R.E. (1993). *Visual communicating.* Englewood Cliffs, NJ: Educational Technology Publications.

Evaluation

Baldwin, T.T. & Ford, J.K. (1988). Transfer of training: A review and directions for future research. *Personnel Psychology, 41*, 63-105.

Broad, M. L. & Newstrom, J. W. (1992). *Transfer of training: Action-packed strategies to ensure high payoff from training investments.* Addison-Wesley Publishing Company.

Butterfield, E.C. & Nelson, G.D. (1989). Theory and practice of teaching for transfer. *Educational Technology Research and Development, 37*(3), 5-38.

Clark, R.E. & Voogel, A. (1985). Transfer of training principles for instructional design. .*Educational Communications and Technology Journal, 33*(2), 113-123.

Flagg, B. N. (Ed.) (1990). *Formative evaluation for educational technologies.* Mahwah, NJ: Lawrence Erlbaum Associates.

Ford, J.K. & Weissbein, D.A. (1997). Transfer of training: An updated review and analysis. *Performance Improvement Quarterly, 10*(2), 22-41.

Foxon, M. (1997). The influence of motivation to transfer, action planning, and manager support on the transfer process. *Performance Improvement Quarterly, 10*(2), 42-63.

Phillips, J. J. (1997). *Handbook of training, evaluation, and measurement methods.* Houston, TX: Gulf Publishing.

Phillips, J. J. (1997). *Return on investment in training and performance improvement programs.* Houston, TX: Gulf Publishing.

Phillips, J.J. (Ed.) (1998). *Implementing Evaluation Systems and Processes.* Alexandria, VA: American Society for Training & Development.

Swanson, R.A. & Holton, E.F. (1999). *Results: How to assess performance, learning, and perceptions in organizations.* San Francisco: Berrett-Koehler Publishers, Inc.

Tannenbaum, S. & Yukl, G. (1992). Training and development in work organizations. *Annual Review of Psychology, 43*, 399-441.

Tessmer, M. (1993). *Planning and conducting formative evaluations.* Bristol, UK: Taylor and Francis.

Quinones, M.A.; Sego, D.J.; Ford, J.K. & Smith, E.M. (1995/1996). The effects of individual and transfer environment characteristics on the opportunity to perform trained tasks. *Training Research Journal, 1*(1), 29-49.

Implementation and Management

Duncan, W.R. (1996). *A guide to the project management body of knowledge.* Newtown Square, PA: Project Management Institute.

Greer. M. (1992). *ID project management: Tools and techniques for instructional designers and developers.* Englewood Cliffs, NJ: Educational Technology Publications.

Greer. M. (1996). *Project manager's partner: A step-by-step guide to project management.* Human Resource Development Press.

Jackson, S. F. & Addison, R.M. (1992). Planning and managing projects. In H.D. Stolovitch and E. J. Keeps (Eds.), *Handbook of human performance technology: A comprehensive guide for analyzing and solving performance problems in organizations* (pp. 66-76). San Francisco: Jossey-Bass.

Rogers, E. M. (1995). *Diffusion of innovations.* New York: The Free Press.

Journals

American Journal of Distance Education
Australian Journal of Educational Technology
British Journal of Educational Technology
Canadian Journal of Educational Communication
Computers and Education
Computers in Human Behavior
Educational Communications and Technology Journal
Educational Computer Magazine
Educational Technology
Educational Technology Research and Development
Human Resource Development Quarterly
Instructional Science
International Journal of Educational Technology
International Journal of Training and Development
Japan Journal of Educational Technology
Journal of Adult Training
Journal of Educational Technology Systems
Journal of European Industrial Training
Learning and Instruction
Performance and Instruction
Performance Improvement Quarterly
Tech Trends
Training
Training and Development Journal
Training Technology
Webnet Journal

The IBSTPI Code of Ethical Standards for Instructional Designers

With J. Michael Spector

I   Guiding Standards: Responsibilities to Others
  A   Provide efficient, effective, workable, and cost-effective solutions to client problems.
  B   Systematically improve human performance to accomplish valid and appropriate individual and organizational goals.
  C   Facilitate individual accomplishment.
  D   Help clients make informed decisions.
  E   Inform others of potential ethical violations and conflicts of interest.
  F   Educate clients in matters of instructional design and performance improvement.

II Guiding Standards: Social Mandates.

   A Support humane, socially responsible goals and activities for individuals and organizations.

   B Make professional decisions based upon moral and ethical positions regarding societal issues.

   C Consider the impact of planned interventions upon individuals, organizations, and the society as a whole.

III Guiding Standards: Respecting the Rights of Others

   A Protect the privacy, candor, and confidentiality of client and colleague information and communication.

   B Show respect for copyright and intellectual property.

   C Do not misuse client or colleague information for personal gain.

   D Do not represent the ideas or work of others as one's own.

   E Do not make false claims about others.

   F Do not discriminate unfairly in actions related to hiring, retention, and advancement.

IV Guiding Standards: Professional Practice

   A Be honest and fair in all facets of one's work.

   B Share skills and knowledge with other professionals.

   C Acknowledge the contributions of others.

   D Aid and be supportive of colleagues.

   E Commit time and effort to the development of the profession.

   F Withdraw from clients who do not act ethically or when there is a conflict of interest.

Organizations Participating in Competency Validation

United States of America – Business, Government, Military

Ameritech

Arthur Andersen

Bandag, Inc.

The Boeing Company

Coopers & Lybrand

Federal Express Corporation

Florida Department of Children and Family Services

Florida Department of Law Enforcement

Florida Department of Revenue

Ford Motor Company

Friesen, Kaye and Associates

Human Performance Technologies of Annapolis

International Business Machines Corporation

Lawson Software

Learning Byte International

Lucent Technologies Inc.
Motorola Inc.
Northwest Airlines Corporation
Price Waterhouse
RWD Technologies Inc.
The Emdicium Group, Inc.
The Operant Group

United States of America – Universities
Arizona State University
Florida State University
San Diego State University
St. Cloud State University
SUNY, Albany
Syracuse University
University of Georgia
University of Minnesota
University of Northern Colorado
University of Oklahoma
University of Pittsburgh
Wayne State University

Europe – Business, Government, Military
Coopers & Lybrand
Dassault Systemes SA
Federal Express Corporation
International Business Machines Corporation
Motorola Inc.
Price Waterhouse

Europe – Universities
Göteborg University
Lancaster University
University of Barcelona
University of Bergen[1]

Asia-Pacific - Business, Government, Military
Arthur Andersen – Singapore & Hong Kong
Australian Army
Australia Defence Force Helicopter School
Coopers & Lybrand –Singapore & Hong Kong
Forge Connexions, Australia
Otec, Australia
Price Waterhouse – Singapore & Hong Kong

Asia-Pacific – Universities
University of Wollongong, Australia

Professional Associations
Kansas City Chapter, International Society for Performance Improvement
Minnesota Chapter, International Society for Performance Improvement
International Consortium for Courseware Engineering

---

[1] The University of Bergen also co-sponsored a conference, "Exploring the Dimensions of Performance Improvement," July 20-21, 1998 at which the draft IBSTPI ID competencies were initially presented and discussed.

LINCOLN CHRISTIAN UNIVERSITY